This book is biblically rich and a[...]
toes in a good way. Again and ag[...]
heart of the matter of marriage: the heart. I gladly commend this work to those who desire to live out a faithful and Christ-centered marriage together.

—**Danny Akin**, President, Southeastern Baptist Theological Seminary

The early years of marriage can be some of the sweetest—and some of the hardest. This book is a gold mine for every young couple! Built on a foundation of the gospel, it offers practical and honest advice on issues such as finances, sexual intimacy, communication, conflict, and more. You don't have to navigate these challenging areas alone. Do your marriage a huge favor and grab a copy of this helpful book.

—**Kristen Clark and Bethany Beal**, Founders, GirlDefined.com; Coauthors, *Girl Defined* and *Love Defined*

Letters to a Romantic: First Years of Marriage is a remarkable resource. It manages to be both extremely practical and persistently gospel focused. The plain, unembarrassed, and open discussions about sex alone are a must-read. But Harmon and Perron go beyond the obvious essentials of sex, money, and in-laws and zoom in as well on matters like hospitality, godly approaches to rest and entertainment, and how to love a spouse who is doubting their faith. Whether you consider yourself a "romantic" or not, this book will strengthen every young marriage—and I can personally report that its wisdom is strengthening at least one older marriage, too!

—**Alasdair Groves**, Executive Director, Christian Counseling and Educational Foundation

In the early years of marriage, the cement of convictions and culture dries quickly. That's why this book is urgently needed. Sean and Spencer have done a masterful job of serving newlyweds—heck, of serving any married couple—by tracing a straight line between the romance that we desire and the beliefs that we should treasure. The result is a tool that will help to build solid foundations for durable marriages.

—**Dave Harvey**, President, Great Commission Collective; Author, *When Sinners Say "I Do"* and *I Still Do*

Sean and Spencer have hit another home run with their third in a series of important books meant to equip couples for the steps of their relationship from dating to marriage. While many books focus on marriage in general, Sean and Spencer have provided an eminently readable, thoroughly biblical, and altogether practical book for couples who are specifically in their first years of marriage. Brimming with wisdom and insight that they have gained from their pastoral and counseling experience, this resource will be one you will surely pass along to young married couples for years to come.

—**Jonathan D. Holmes**, Founder and Executive Director, Fieldstone Counseling; Pastor of Counseling, Parkside Church, Chagrin Falls, Ohio; Author, *Counsel for Couples: A Biblical and Practical Guide for Marriage Counseling*

As they have in their other volumes, Sean and Spencer root the realities of romance in Scripture's relevance for daily life. Seasoned by their early years of marriage, these two men are desperate for you to taste of the richness of God's Word, which has proven itself to be a sturdy and strong foundation for marriage. With pastoral clarity, they help young couples to consider the importance of the patterns and rhythms they establish in their early years and to make them a worthy investment that will help their later years to be all the more sweet. I can say, as someone who has been married for twenty years and now has six children, that their advice is wise beyond their years and provides a practical guide for true romance that will flourish and sweeten with every passing year.

—**T. Dale Johnson**, Executive Director, Association of Certified Biblical Counselors; Associate Professor of Biblical Counseling, Midwestern Baptist Theological Seminary

This book is rich wisdom about the complex situations that surround the first year of marriage. Its words come from faithful men who have walked this road with grace and are eager to pass on what they have learned to you. This resource is an investment in your marriage that will pay dividends for decades.

—**Heath Lambert**, Senior Pastor, First Baptist Church,
Jacksonville, Florida

This book for newlyweds is needed and tremendously helpful. It contains timely challenges and encouragements as well as relevant instructions for people at every stage of marriage, though its material is especially relevant for newlyweds. Having been in ministry and having had the privilege of performing the premarital counseling as well as the weddings of numerous people over the past sixty-two years, I wish that this book had been available to give to all these couples as they began their marriages. Marriages that begin right are much more likely to continue right. And I highly recommend this book as a vital part of that good beginning.

—**Wayne Mack**, Academic Head, Strengthening Ministries
Training Institute; Director, Association of Certified Biblical
Counselors—Africa

This book wisely addresses the most significant challenges that many young Christian married couples face in a way that is both practical and biblical. My wife and I are eager to give this resource to the young husbands and wives whom we have been counseling. It is fun to read and would make a great couples' devotional.

—**Jim Newheiser**, Director of the Christian Counseling Program
and Associate Professor of Christian Counseling and Pastoral
Theology, Reformed Theological Seminary

This book combines biblical instruction and practical observations made by men who are discovering how to build a marriage for the long haul. I believe nearlyweds and newlyweds will find it especially helpful. My favorite aspect of this book is the enthusiasm, passion, and positivity about marriage and family that permeate every page.

—**Jimmy Scroggins**, Lead Pastor, Family Church, West Palm Beach

The patterns of the first few months of married life soon—for better or worse—harden into habits. These habits set trajectories that can take a couple far from where they want to be in many areas of their relationship. This book can help to break bad habits in a marriage and then reshape them into routines that are more glorifying to God and satisfying to a couple.

—**Donald S. Whitney**, Professor of Biblical Spirituality and Associate Dean for the School of Theology, The Southern Baptist Theological Seminary

letters

TO A

Romantic

Also by Sean Perron and Spencer Harmon

Letters to a Romantic: On Dating
Letters to a Romantic: On Engagement

Letters

TO A

Romantic

FIRST YEARS OF MARRIAGE

SEAN PERRON
& SPENCER HARMON

P&R
PUBLISHING
P.O. BOX 817 • PHILLIPSBURG • NEW JERSEY 08865-0817

Printed in the United States of America

Library of Congress Cataloging-in-Publication Data

Names: Perron, Sean, author. | Harmon, Spencer, author.
Title: Letters to a romantic : first years of marriage / Sean Perron and
   Spencer Harmon.
Description: Phillipsburg, New Jersey : P&R Publishing Company, 2020. |
   Summary: "The first years of a marriage set patterns that can determine
   its course for decades. Warm and practical, Sean and Spencer give
   biblical wisdom and address everyday details and concerns"-- Provided by
   publisher.
Identifiers: LCCN 2020008897 | ISBN 9781629954653 (paperback) | ISBN
   9781629954660 (epub) | ISBN 9781629955582 (mobi)
Subjects: LCSH: Married people--Religious life. | Newlyweds--Religious
   life. | Marriage--Religious aspects--Christianity.
Classification: LCC BV4596.M3 P47 2020 | DDC 248.8/44--dc23
LC record available at https://lccn.loc.gov/2020008897

To my parents:

I praise God for your faithfulness to each other.

—Sean

To Melody, Harper, and Wally:

You have filled our early years with joy.

—Spencer

CONTENTS

FOREWORD

Letters to a Romantic: First Years of Marriage is a unique book. Even though there are many books on marriage issues, they are not specific for newlywed couples. The chapters in this book cover twenty-two relevant issues and answer the questions that almost all newlyweds wonder about.

Each chapter is warm and inviting due to its letter format. The chapters are easy for each couple to personalize. The chapters are brief, and both husband and wife would benefit greatly if they read and discuss each chapter together. Additionally, each brief chapter contains discussion questions at the end, thus making it easy for them to see their strengths as well as their weaknesses that need work.

Harmon and Perron are both young pastors and have been trained as biblical counselors. Both have been married for over five years and have children. So they know firsthand what the first five years are like from their own lives as well as from the couples they have counseled. Thus, they take the reader on a contemplative stroll up and down the aisle of relevant topics they may face. Their chapters are full of very practical applications that are based on specific Scriptures.

The chapters are Christ-centered, and it is obvious that both authors have a very high view of God. They remind the reader that everyday, ordinary married life is an opportunity to either honor God or steal his glory. Some days, your marriage may be difficult and you may feel discouraged; but remember that even on the most difficult days, it is always an opportunity to glorify God and show love to your spouse. This book reminds you of the many special opportunities you have to do this.

Its topics are immensely practical—parents, sex, children, money, church, impurity in marriage, suffering, and even doubting God. Each brief chapter stands by itself, and in pertinent chapters Harmon and Perron have teamed with their wives to obtain a more balanced view.

Walking the reader through God's relevant and sufficient Word on these issues, Harmon and Perron have developed an effective tool for couples and for those counseling newlyweds. This will be a very valuable tool in the biblical counselor's toolbox.

We recommend this book to you and pray that God will bless each reader to the praise of His glory and grace.

Martha Peace
Stuart Scott
June 2020

INTRODUCTION

HOW TO THINK ABOUT
THE FIRST YEARS

Sean and Spencer

Dear Romantic,

Why should you listen to two guys who aren't even thirty talk about the early years of marriage?

Neither of us has been married for longer than ten years. There is still a lot of marriage for us to experience. We are young pastors at the beginning of ministry. Our kids are young. We have just exited the "first years of marriage" ourselves. Shouldn't we not bother with writing a book and simply keep our heads down while those who have more years under their belts speak to these issues?

Those questions are the very reason we wrote this book.

We know we have blind spots and immaturities—you'll read about many of them in the coming pages. As we write these letters to you, we aren't pretending to be marriage experts. That's why these chapters are relatively short—you'll find a resource section in the back listing books that have been written by those much wiser than we are.

Yet we believe there is an advantage to writing a book from right on the "other side" of the early years of marriage. Most books on marriage are aimed at addressing timeless problems with timeless truths that are found in Scripture. This is always needed. But we also recognize that people gain unique help from listening to those who have just walked through the same season they are in. The early years of marriage involve unique struggles and opportunities that are easy to forget by the time someone is three decades into marriage.

Picture us, then, not as veterans of marriage who are sharing sage stories of years long past. Instead, think of us as fellow soldiers in the trenches who have been here a few years longer than you have. We want to share with you what we have learned since we've gotten here, some pitfalls to watch out for, and a weapon that is absolutely necessary if you want to make it to victory.

That weapon, of course, is the Bible.

We believe that the Bible, not us, is a sufficient source of marriage advice. That means that age and experience are important, but the helpfulness of any marriage advice should be determined by how faithfully it reflects God's Word—not whether or not it comes from someone who has been married for a long time. You can have wrinkles and yet no wisdom, and you can also be young and have lots of it. God's Word is what makes the difference (see Ps. 119:99–101)

Our goal in this book is not to point you to ourselves, our experience, or our advice. Our goal is to point you away from ourselves and to the only source of real help: Jesus Christ as he is revealed in Scripture.

We wrote this book on the first years of marriage with the later years of marriage also in view. These years are deeply influential.

The way you talk and think about sex and children and money and conflict now influences the way you'll be talking about these things on your thirtieth anniversary. We want those conversations to be shaped by Scripture and conformed to Christ.

As you read, you will notice that our wives have cosigned many of the letters. The teaching of kindness is on their tongues (see Prov. 31:26), and their wisdom has permeated this book. Their tone and tenderness have blessed our writing, and their thoughtful additions are words fitly spoken (see Prov. 25:11).

Our prayer is that, as you read, you will hear the familiar words of the person who is most qualified to talk about marriage—Jesus Christ (who never married)—and will forget all about us. And we also pray that, as we all listen to him, our marriages would look more and more Christlike during the first years and every year that follows.

Until then,
Sean and Spencer

WHEN MARRIAGE
EXPOSES YOUR HEART

Spencer

Dear Romantic,

Marriage is an experiment in exposure. Every day, you are more exposed to your spouse—to his or her character, quirks, rhythm of life, sin, and struggles. This isn't shocking. You married a dynamic saint-and-yet-sinner who both strives and stumbles (see Col. 3:9–10) and whose dreams, preferences, and habits are developing throughout these first years of marriage.

What's more jarring, though, is how marriage exposes *you.* Your preferences, decisions, and convictions now have a direct and sustained impact on another person—your spouse. Too often that impact can leave your spouse feeling hurt and you feeling confused. How did we get here? Marriage unearths the deep roots of our hearts, and we can often be discouraged at what we find.

Our hearts are the control centers of all the *beliefs, values,* and *commitments* that we carry into every area of our lives— things that directly impact how we relate to God, others, and our circumstances.[1] The question is not *if*, but *how*, our hearts impact our marriages—and we need to be willing to evaluate them in the light of Scripture.

OUR HEARTS IN MARRIAGE

It's tempting to think that all the problems you face in these early years come from the *outside*—from your spouse, your circumstances, your resources. But Jesus locates all these problems on the inside: "For *out of the heart* come evil thoughts, murder, adultery, sexual immorality, theft, false witness, slander. These are what defile a person" (Matt. 15:19–20).

Jesus doesn't say that our anger, envy, discontent, or laziness *happens* to us because of some *real* problem such as a foolish boss, lack of money, or stressful schedule. Instead, he wants us to see these issues as mirrors that reflect a deeper problem in our hearts—sin. If you have been married for more than a week, you have probably seen all kinds of problems in your marriage that you want to change. Jesus wants you to know where they come from.

But Jesus doesn't just want us to know the source of these issues so that we can feel bad about how sinful we are. He shows us our hearts so that our marriages can, when we have faith in his gospel, bear fruit for his glory.

THE HEART OF MARRIAGE

We can't figure out marriage on our own—any more than we are called to cleanse our sinful hearts on our own. Only Jesus

---

1. This definition of our hearts is deeply influenced by Jeremy Pierre's excellent book, *The Dynamic Heart in Daily Life: Connecting Christ to Human Experience* (Greensboro, NC: New Growth Press, 2016).

has the resources that we need if we are going to bear fruit in our marriages. This means that we must look at the sin in our hearts that bears fruit in our marriages and then *trust* Jesus for the forgiveness he makes available through his death on the cross and resurrection from the dead. It also means *continuing to trust* Jesus for power over sin in our marriages.

If you have realized that you can't do marriage on your own, take comfort—Jesus knew this and has given you a promise to soothe your soul. He tells you that your heart will not produce fruit unless you abide in him—that apart from him you can do nothing (see John 15:4–5). We *need him* and his gospel. We need forgiveness for our sinful hearts through the cross, and we need faith so we can root our marriages in him every day.

This is why Paul's marriage advice grows out of the gospel message itself. Husbands take their cues from the way that Christ relates to his people—he is the leader who humbly lays down his life for the good of his wife (see Eph. 5:25). Wives take their cues from the way that the church relates to Christ—they submit themselves to their husbands' good leadership, just as the church follows Jesus (see Eph. 5:24).

Only Jesus is able to address the complex problems that we face in these first years of marriage. And, as we abide in Jesus as he is revealed to us in the gospel, not only do we find solutions to our problems, but we also display that sufficient gospel for the whole world to see.

ALIGNING OUR HEARTS

My hope for you as I write this book is that your marriage would grow and bear fruit. That happens when your *heart* believes God's Word and when you act on it in every area of your life. You're going to get a lot of practical advice in this book. My hope is that it will help you to change. But in order for any of us to experience change that is rooted in the *gospel*, there are at least three steps we need to take.

Naming the sin in our hearts. One of the biggest temptations we face in the early years of marriage is to minimize our sin or to call it something different from what Jesus does in his Word. We reconceive our rebellion against God as merely an "inconvenience" to our happiness or to the happiness of our spouses. Be committed instead to agreeing with Christ about the sin that you bring into your marriage. Jesus promises forgiveness for and power over *sin*—not inconveniences.

Hating the sin that we find in our hearts. One of the signs that we have repented of our sin is that we *hate it* for what it is—sin against God. Our hearts must be motivated not just by a desire to get problems out of our lives but by a desire to display the gospel in our marriages.

Replacing the sin that we find in our hearts. The call of Christ is not primarily for us to develop a refined sense of our own sinfulness. His primary call is for us to repent of our sin and put on faith in Christ (see Gal. 2:20). This means believing God's Word and applying it to problems in our marriages.

As you seek to grow, strengthen, and change in your marriage, my hope is that you would be rooted in the gospel. Only the gospel can expose your deepest problem—your sin—and then provide the only solution that leads to lasting change.

Marriage is an experiment in exposure. God designed it that way. But the beauty of this design is that even as marriage exposes painful things about us, it also exposes the way in which

Christ, his grace, and the gospel uniquely address all the problems we face.

Until then,
Spencer

DISCUSSION QUESTIONS

1. In what ways has marriage exposed you? Be specific.
2. What is harder—trusting Jesus to forgive you of your sin or trusting Jesus for the power to change? Why? Discuss this with your spouse.
3. This chapter lists three components of biblical change. Which of them is hardest for you? Why?

SHOULD WE GO TO CHURCH?

Spencer

Dear Romantic,

I love coming home. When I'm tired after a long day of work, I love walking through the door and seeing my family who love me, know me, and share life with me.

Coming home doesn't solve my every problem—my family has its problems, too! But it provides me with a place where my joys and burdens are shared and carried. It refreshes me, rejuvenates me, and reminds me of what is important. It's a place that often gives me exactly what I need in order to go back out into the world and be faithful throughout everyday life.

Now, I want you to think of the local church that way.

Have you noticed that there are no books of the Bible dedicated to couples? All the marriage advice that we read in the New Testament is given in the context of the local church. Paul gives advice on sex within marriage in a letter to a church in Corinth (see 1 Cor. 7:3–5). He explains the mystery of marriage in a letter to another church in Ephesus (see Eph. 5:22–33). He also gives practical advice to couples who are in a congregation in Colossae (see Col. 3:18–19). Likewise, Peter writes about roles in marriage to a group of churches (see 1 Peter 3:1–7).

God designed your marriage to be deeply connected to the life of the local church. Our church is the place where we are reminded of truth, refreshed in the gospel, and rejuvenated for our mission. It should be the place where a couple seeks to glorify God. It's the most important arena for the early years of our marriage to play out.

And it's also the most neglected.

Maybe you are confused by this description of the church. Church seems more like a tax on your marriage than a benefit. You might have grown up in church and thought that it seemed full of angry, bored, private people who came out of obligation. If you have tried church since you've been a couple, maybe you haven't been able to connect with other people who are in your season of life and marriage. Or perhaps this is the first time you have even thought about going to church as a couple.

Whatever your relationship with church may be, I want you to know that God wants his local church to be the context in which your marriage is grown and refreshed.

WHERE A MARRIAGE IS GROWN

The best place for a garden to grow is where there is good soil and plenty of sun and water. The most valuable crops are planted where they will receive what they need in order to grow strong. God has designed his church to be the place where your marriage should grow.

I'm not saying that if you go to church every Sunday, you will automatically have a wonderful marriage. Bad churches can harm your marriage, and there are ways that you can "go to church" without growing. But that doesn't change what God's design is for his church.

God is bringing together a diverse family of people who are united by faith in the gospel and through the death and resurrection of Christ. This is the church—the family of God. And God promises his church that he will grow it.

There is no such thing as a Christian (or a Christian marriage) that grows without having a deep connection to the church (see Eph. 2:19–22). It's where all the action is happening.

At church, you and your spouse will hear the Bible every week. It is where you will be reminded of the message of the gospel that your marriage is meant to portray. You will pray and be prayed for; and, God willing, you will be spiritually refreshed and grown.

WHERE A MARRIAGE IS KNOWN

Maybe you're like me—you regularly look for "silver bullet" resources. If you have some problems in your marriage, you start looking for help—some missing piece of insight, some pithy phrase, some helpful how-to advice that will solve your unique problem overnight.

What we are looking for when we do this is for someone to know us, and to speak into our lives and marriages based on the knowledge that they have about us. This is exactly what God has provided for us inside the local church. Paul calls all the members of the church to lovingly speak into one another's lives so that all of us grow in *every area* and *every way*: "Speaking the truth in love, we are to grow up in every way into him who is the head, into Christ, from whom the whole body, joined and held together by every joint with which it is equipped, when each part is working properly, makes the body grow so that it builds itself up in love" (Eph. 4:15–16).

The local church is one of God's primary resources for blessing our marriages. It is where you are connected with other Christians who love you and can wisely apply the truth of God's Word to your marriage. It is where your new marriage can be uniquely *known* and lovingly helped by other members. In God's design, the local church is meant to be a place where you are regularly asked, "How's your marriage going?"

WHERE A MARRIAGE IS GUARDED

Problems appear in my marriage when I get spiritually sleepy. I become embittered about sacrificially serving at home if my heart isn't awake to Christ's sacrifice for me (see Eph. 5:25). My heart becomes hard toward my wife when it isn't soft toward the grace of Christ (see Col. 3:12–13). Most of the problems in our marriages stem not from turning our backs on God's Word outright but from slowly drifting from it.

God designed his church to guard our marriages against lethargically drifting from his Word. He has given his church to our marriages so that we will always have brothers and sisters to tell us, "Wake up!" when our eyes start to glaze: "But exhort one another every day, as long as it is called 'today,' that none of you may be hardened by the deceitfulness of sin" (Heb. 3:13).

We are prone to wander, and God has provided the local church to keep us near to our Good Shepherd. One of the reasons we show up and gather with God's people every week is so that we can regularly be reminded of the grace God has shown us in Christ and can turn away from sin.

MAKING YOUR CHURCH FEEL LIKE HOME

How can we make the local church a home that will grow us, know us, and guard us? Here are four basic steps.

Become members of a Bible-preaching church. If you attend a church already but are not an official member of it, take that step of commitment. If you do not attend a church, this is the perfect opportunity to find one in your community that opens the Bible every week, preaches what it says, and applies the message of the gospel to all of life—and then to commit to it. Don't be flaky. Become a member, let the pastors shepherd you, and serve the other members. Taking this step of commitment and membership will help to make the church your family.

Show up every week. Your closest friends are your closest friends because you have invested in your relationship with them over a long period of time. You have regular rhythms of talking with and seeing one another. Apply that same sort of relational commitment to your local church—even if you don't feel close to everyone in it right away. Be intentional about showing up every week. Make it a nonnegotiable in your family that, unless someone is sick or you are out of town, you will be in your local church every week.

Find a godly couple. Most local churches will have at least one husband and wife who are older than you. Cultivate a relationship with them, and let them invest in you. Have them over for dinner. Ask them questions. Be honest.

Be open and humble. I have found that my relationships in my church thrive the most when I am open and vulnerable about how I am struggling in my marriage and when I humbly receive the encouragement of others. When a person asks you, "How is marriage going?" you should make a point of giving them the real answer. You'll be surprised at how God grows and helps you through their words.

My prayer is that the local church won't be some extracurricular activity for you and your spouse. Instead, I'm praying that the local church becomes one of the central places where your marriage plays out, grows, and serves others. God designed it to be that way. As you commit yourself to God's design, you will find refreshment, joy, and direction that will bless your marriage for a lifetime.

Until then,
Spencer

DISCUSSION QUESTIONS

1. When was the last time you felt refreshed at church? Why?
2. Discuss with your spouse the ways in which your marriage is "spiritually sleepy."
3. Think of a couple in your church whose marriage you both admire. What do you admire about it? Make a plan to invite that couple over for dinner.
4. What step could you take next to become more committed to your local church (e.g., membership, serving in a ministry, joining a Sunday school or community group)? Write it down and make a plan to take it.

GETTING HELP IN
YOUR MARRIAGE

Sean and Jenny

Dear Romantic,

A plague is sweeping our country. It is a deadly disease with many fatalities. Thousands of marriages have died because of it, and it has left many more marriages in continual pain, misery, and suffering. Do you know what this lethal disease is?

Not asking for help.

Do you shudder when you read that? You should. You should tremble. Not asking for help kills marriages every day. It is a cancer for couples—a leprosy for lovers.

And the worst part of the whole epidemic is that many couples neglect the fact that . . . there is a cure.

There is an effective treatment for couples who have this disease.

All they have to do is ask.

It is easy for us, as married couples, to avoid assistance. We can go home, close the front door, and deal with things; and no one has to know. But Jesus does not intend for the Christian life to be one of solitude and isolated fortitude (see Eccl. 4:9–12). He wants us to walk together in community.

Jesus doesn't want couples to deal with difficulties all by themselves. We all need help, and we are called to help one another (see Eph. 4:14–16). The church is designed for these exact needs.

COUPLES DELAY

One of the errors many married couples make is waiting too long to get help from the church.[1] Couples delay until things are really bad. They unfortunately reserve the option of getting help for only cataclysmic marriage issues.

Instead of delaying, you should adopt the posture "When in doubt, let's check it out." If you find a lump, get it examined. If it is nothing at all, then that's good to know! If it is cancerous, then be even more thankful that you got it looked at! The sooner you get things assessed, the better. And the same applies to issues in your marriage. It never hurts to ask someone who is wiser to examine your life together.

Your marriage needs help just like your car needs maintenance. Even if you get a brand-new car, you still need to take it to the shop for oil changes, tire rotations, and other alignments. If you never take your vehicle in for an inspection, you are irresponsible to your own detriment. And by the same token, it is a good practice to regularly have more mature Christians check in on your relationship.

---

1. If you are in a church that preaches the gospel, you should reach out to one of your pastors for help. There will also be older godly couples who would love to talk with you. If they tell you that they are not equipped to help you, you can find a certified biblical counselor at www.biblicalcounseling.com. For details about how to find biblical counseling, see the recommended resource page at the end of this book.

When was the last time that you and your spouse took your marriage in for a checkup? When was the last time you had dinner with a godly couple from church and asked them to speak into your life? When a godly couple speaks into your life, it is like a skilled gardener tending a backyard. You will flourish when someone comes to pull the weeds of sin from your marriage and to do a little pruning on the areas that need direction.

COUPLES DENY

Coworker: "How are you guys doing?"
Us: "Doing fine."

Church member: "How's it going?"
Us: "Great."

Asking questions like this is a typical way for us to greet one another in our culture. But the responses that we give back to such questions are usually a polite lie. We say that things are great when they aren't. We say things are fine when they are far from it. Don't be the couple who deny reality.

Spouses who deny their problems publicly are often too embarrassed to ask for help. Maybe you are introverted. Maybe you are nervous that the whole church will discover your problems. Maybe you have built up a reputation, and this would ruin it. Maybe you come from a family that never spoke about problems and never sought out help.

No matter what your reason is for denying your own problems, it isn't good enough. Really. Whatever excuses you're making or embarrassment you might feel don't outweigh the effects that will result from staying quiet and alone.

When Jesus said that only the sick need a doctor, he was

addressing the Pharisees. They were sick just like everyone else, but they thought they were healthy. Ironically, they were the most disease-ridden of all—and it killed them. In their pride, they perished. But the prostitutes and tax collectors made it to the ER and had successful surgery (see Matt. 21:31–32). Jesus did not come to save "the righteous"; he came to save sinners (see Mark 2:17). So if we are to experience healing in our marriages, we must admit that we have a problem and that we are part of it.[2]

Do you think that you are the only couple who have doubts about whether their relationship is working? Do you think that you are the only married couple who struggle with anger, bitterness, and resentment? Do you think that you are the only person who isn't sexually satisfied or content in marriage?

The Bible says there is nothing new under the sun (see Eccl. 1:9)—and that is good news for you. Jesus isn't shocked by your problems, because no temptation has overcome you except what is common to man (see 1 Cor. 10:13). Bring your dilemmas into the light. You will be surprised to learn how many other people have struggled with the same things as you.

COUPLES DOWNPLAY

Closely related to the common practice of delaying or denying help is the problem of downplaying the need for it. Couples underestimate the seriousness of their issues. Spouses think their marriage problems will fix themselves. But they won't.

As I was working on this book, our air conditioning went out

2. In this chapter I am not addressing any issues related to abuse, suicide, or physical danger. If you are in physical danger, you should reach out immediately to the proper authorities and get the help you need. For more on the importance of safety in an abusive marriage, see the resources listed at the back of this book.

in our vehicle. It made a rattling noise, and then the air wasn't as cold as it should have been. We thought that maybe if we did nothing, it would eventually come back on. We drove around for a couple of days, and the air was still lukewarm. You might be able to get away with lukewarm air in another state . . . but not in Florida . . . not in July.

The more we drove, the more our wishful thinking about the air returning continued to evaporate—unlike the sweat coming off our bodies. We finally decided that it was too much when the AC became even warmer than the weather outside! We had to admit that our car wasn't going to fix itself.

Are there any issues in your marriage that you are hoping will just fix themselves?

- "This lust will eventually go away. I can handle it."
- "I'm not bringing that up again. It isn't that big a deal. We will move on."
- "She'll forget about that, I'm sure."
- "I don't know what to say. He doesn't seem all that bothered by it anyway."

Delaying, denying, and downplaying the help that we need are all variants of the same disease.

Pride.

The medicine that all (and I mean *all*) marriages need is humility.

We need the humility of broken prostitutes and repentant tax collectors (see Luke 18:13).

Humility is the key to finding hope and healing. If we admit that we need something, we can then ask Jesus for help. God loves to get glory by helping weak, broken, and sinful people.

There is great hope that comes when we confess. A friend

once said, "It is good to make yourself look bad on this day in order to look good in Christ on the last day."

God opposes the proud but gives grace to the humble (see James 4:6). The proud find only opposition and pain. The humble receive grace and relief. What are you waiting for? Reach out today to a trusted couple in your church—and to our precious Christ who died for us.

> Come, ye weary, heavy laden,
> Lost and ruined by the fall;
> If you tarry till you're better,
> You will never come at all.
> I will arise and go to Jesus,
> He will embrace me in His arms;
> In the arms of my dear Savior,
> O, there are ten thousand charms.[3]

Please don't tarry till you're better. Arise, ask for help, and go to Jesus. He will embrace you in his arms.

Until then,
Sean and Jenny

DISCUSSION QUESTIONS

1. When you have a problem in your marriage, what are you tempted to do? Deny getting help? Delay getting help? Or downplay the help that you need?

3. Joseph Hart, "Come Ye Sinners, Poor and Needy," 1759; with amendments by Augustus Toplady, 1776; and an anonymously authored refrain.

2. Are you nervous or embarrassed about reaching out for help? If so, why?

3. When was the last time you asked your spouse to give you an honest assessment of how you are doing in your marriage?

4. Who are the godly couples who are speaking into your life and marriage? If you don't have any, then who can you invite into your life?

WHAT ARE THE ROLES OF
A HUSBAND AND WIFE?

Spencer and Taylor

Dear Romantic,

Imagine that your marriage is a drama, and your life is the theater.

You and your spouse both have roles to play. You have a script. You have lines. You have cues. The roles that both of you play are equally crucial to the story that is unfolding throughout the drama. If one actor breaks character or refuses to follow the script, the story is interrupted and the drama is diluted. If the audience is going to be caught up in the story, the actors must be committed to the parts they have been given to play.

The picture of marriage as a drama is not far off from the way Scripture talks about the roles of a husband and wife in marriage. Both play a role that takes its cues from the gospel. Marriage is an enormous and privileged opportunity for a husband and wife to uniquely display the beauty of the gospel itself.

This is crucial to understand, because the prospect of both genders having separate roles in marriage is regularly seen as a threat rather than an opportunity. Gender roles are seen as being a restraint to men—and especially to women. But this idea is foreign to Scripture. Scripture calls husbands and wives to play complementary roles in the theater of life in order to display the glorious story of Jesus and the church.

OUR WORTH DOES NOT LIE IN WHAT WE DO

Our world sees the gender roles within marriage as a threat because it often equates our worth as human beings with what we do. You haven't "made it" in your job until you get to the top. The people whom we prize are people who hustle. We must master our craft, excel past our peers, beat the odds. We lift up people who "aren't like everyone else," and we find worth in carving our own paths.

But the Bible liberates us from this perspective. Instead of locating our value in what we do, Scripture ties our value to our Creator who made us (see Gen. 1:27; 9:6; James 3:8–9). That means that *all people* have equal value before God simply because they were created by him. Our dignity is permanent. Our value is safe, and no one can threaten it.

This is crucial for you to understand as you seek to live out God's design for your marriage in the early years. God's script for the role you play in marriage isn't an assessment of your value. It's your instructions for glorifying him in the most significant relationship of your life.

So, then, what are the roles within this drama of marriage?

THE HUSBAND'S SCRIPT: LOVING AUTHORITY

Husbands are called to exercise loving authority in marriage. This is what Paul means when he says in Ephesians 5:23 that "the husband is the head of the wife even as Christ is the head of the church."[1] This means that husbands are the primary leaders of, providers for, and protectors of their families.

Brothers, this doesn't mean that we use our authority to flex and bend everything in our homes to our preferences. We don't use our authority to control what's for dinner every night and what channel everyone watches on TV or to make our wives feel like employees. No, it means that we use our authority like Jesus does—to love and to give. "Husbands, *love* your wives, as Christ *loved* the church and *gave* himself up for her" (Eph. 5:25).

Let's put it this way: your authority should be *good news* for your wife. The practical result when men exercise loving authority in their marriages is that their wives feel *nourished* and *cherished* (see Eph. 5:29).

Our wives should know that we're aiming to use our authority to nourish them every day. This means we make sure that food stays on the table, the Bible remains open, and our lives move toward the same goal. It means that it should be abundantly obvious to our wives that we cherish them more than we do sports, or books, or work, or ministry, or our friends. Even when we must make hard leadership decisions, we should work hard to make sure our wives know we are aiming for their good.

Maybe you've never seen an example of this. Don't let it stay that way. Ask your pastor to point you in the direction of men who lead their homes and cherish their families. Invite yourself over for dinner—and watch.

The authority of the husband is marked by the same servant leadership that our Savior exhibited. Its symbol is a cross, not a power tie.

1. For a detailed exegetical, theological, and historical argument for this teaching, read John Piper and Wayne Grudem, *Recovering Biblical Manhood*

THE WIFE'S SCRIPT: WORSHIPFUL SUBMISSION

Wives are called to submit to their own husbands: "Wives, submit to your own husbands, as to the Lord" (Eph. 5:22). This means that the wife follows the lead of her husband as an act of worship to the Lord.

This is a picture before it is a practice. Sisters, we must be members of Jesus's church and see how it submits to him before we seek to reenact that submission in our marriages. The fruit of submission in the life of a wife grows from a heart that is deeply rooted in the gospel it is called to portray. We need this, because we can't simply submit out of duty. Submission doesn't come from a grin-and-bear-it attitude. It must become a delight to us— one that we ignite by beholding our great Savior who loves us and gave himself for us (see Gal. 2:20). This reorients our hearts from seeking motivation from the quality of our husbands' leadership to seeking to trust our loving heavenly Father. It results in our respecting the authority of our husbands because we trust that God's plan for our marriages is better than our own. Our hearts must delight in the picture he calls us to display before we practice the role that he calls us to play.

Since submission is an act of worship to God, it means that we should be *eager* to practice it in marriage. In these first years, the shortcomings of your husband's leadership will become more and more clear. Every wife must ask herself, Will I be eager to find ways that my husband is failing to lead or will I be eager to find ways that I can joyfully follow? Will I judge my husband for failures to lead or will I encourage the ways that I see him growing in leadership? Will I respect my husband and

---

and Womanhood: A Response to Evangelical Feminism (1991; repr., Wheaton, IL: Crossway, 2012).

the role God has given him in the grand drama or will I despise that role?

CONCLUSION

Marriage—along with our roles in it—isn't about us. It's a small picture of something greater that is coming. One day, the church will be presented without blemish to Jesus (see Eph. 5:26–27; Rev. 19:6–8), and our imperfect marriages will fade away (see Matt. 22:30). We should always keep this perspective in view as we live out our roles today. We are the opening act for the greater story of God's love for his people. As husbands and wives, we set the stage and prepare the way for the greater drama we will celebrate for all eternity.

Until then,
Spencer and Taylor

DISCUSSION QUESTIONS

1. Do you struggle with thinking that gender roles are a threat? Why?
2. Brother, ask your wife if she thinks you are using your position of authority in your marriage to serve. What is her answer—and what are her reasons for saying so?
3. Sister, ask your husband if he thinks you focus more on his leadership shortcomings or on the ways he is growing. What is his answer—and what are his reasons for saying so?
4. What are some ways that you struggle to apply your role in your daily life?

FREEDOM IN MARRIAGE

Spencer and Taylor

Dear Romantic,

I don't do the laundry or cook much in our home. I don't decorate. I don't do a lot of grocery shopping—or much shopping at all, for that matter. You want to know why I don't do these things? It's not because the Bible says I can't. Here's why:

I stink at them.

Ask my wife. The last time I tried to do the laundry, she sent me a text message the next day that said, "You're not allowed to do laundry anymore. I love you." If you asked me to take over details like this for our family, our main diet would be frozen pizza, grilled cheese, and creative renditions of pancakes-for-dinner. The walls of our home would be white and bare. And my cute daughters would wear a rotation of three or four outfits—all with the same ponytail.

My wife does laundry, cooks dinner, and decorates our home beautifully not for primarily theological reasons. It's practical. She does them because she's better at them than I am. I manage our money and budget. She plans meals. She decorates the house. I do the dishes.

I'm sharing all of this with you for a reason. Whenever conversations about gender roles happen, a common misunderstanding emerges: that if each of us has been given a role and a script in the grand drama of marriage, this must mean that there is no room for variation in the way we flesh out that role in our homes. This means that submission looks the same for every woman and that leadership looks the same for every man—down to the small details that play out in their homes.

But any good performer will tell you that what makes a performance authentic is when actors make it their own. While they stick to their lines and cues, they play the role in a way that only they could.

What kind of freedom are you and your spouse allowed regarding the way you fulfill your God-given roles in your marriage? There are three common areas to which you need to apply this question in your first years of marriage.

THE DETAILS OF THE HOME

Who mops the floor? Who cooks dinner? Who vacuums? Who dusts? Who feeds the dog? Who takes out the trash? Who washes the clothes? Who folds the laundry and puts it away? Who pays the insurance bill every month? Who manages the family calendar and invites the new neighbor family over for a BBQ?

You decide. The Bible doesn't say what specific household tasks need to be done by each spouse. Instead, it tells you that men are called to lead and nourish and cherish their wives and that women are called to honor and submit to their husbands (see Eph. 5:22–33; 1 Peter 3:1–6). Your call is to set up your home in the way that most faithfully enables both of you to fulfill these roles.

Biblically, both husband and wife are to have a vested interest in the home. Fathers aren't called to check out when they get home; they are called to engage. This is what Paul implies when he calls dads to be the disciplers of their children (see Eph. 6:4). Women are called to "love their husbands and children, to be self-controlled, pure, *working at home*, kind, and submissive to their own husbands" (Titus 2:4–5).

Men should care about the home. You can't manage what you don't know. If the daily chores of the home aren't getting done, a husband should initiate a conversation with his wife and kids so they can all set up a way to get the work done. When this happens, women should partner with their husbands to enact this plan to get the work done.

Each couple might divide the particulars of their rhythm differently, but both husband and wife have a vested interest in it. There is no room for indifference.

THE DYNAMICS OF WORK

You may have circled that Titus quotation above and put a little question mark in the margin. If women are supposed to be "working at home," does that mean they may never work outside the home?

When the Bible talks about the work that women do, it primarily has the home in focus. This is what Paul has in mind when he says, in that quotation from Titus, that older women are to train younger women to be "working at home" and when he envisions the remarried young widow "managing [her] household" (1 Tim. 5:14).

This does not mean that couples never have space to improvise in this area. Some men are unable to fully provide for their families through their current work, and their wives are called to partner with them and work in order to make ends meet. I have known couples who agree for a season for the wife to be the primary breadwinner while the husband goes to graduate school. The goal behind an arrangement like this is for the husband to be better equipped to provide for the family in the future.

But what about a wife who desires to be out in the workforce? Is she forced to "stay home" instead of pursuing meaningful work outside the house? No. Proverbs 31:16–18 gives us a portrait of a woman working outside the home—one who purchases a field, plants a vineyard, and is marked by strength and savvy business practices.

But it's important to notice that the woman in Proverbs 31 does all these things while still faithfully looking after her home. She is looking well to the ways of her household, and her children and husband bless her (see vv. 27–28). She works outside her home—not to the neglect of her role as a wife (and, if she has children, as a mother) but to the benefit of it.

THE DUTIES OF FAMILY

Dads are specifically charged with bringing up their children in the discipline and instruction of the Lord (see Eph. 6:4). This means that God has charged fathers to *train* their children—to help them to see the world through the lens of the Bible and to direct them onto a wise path before they launch out of the home. Yet moms are also called to a crucial role in the raising of children. We see in the Bible that, by all appearances, Timothy's faith was passed down primarily through his mom (see 2 Tim. 1:5) and that sons are commanded to listen to their mothers' teaching (see Prov. 1:8).

This means that husbands should be the *initiators* in the training and disciplining of their children, but both husbands and wives are to actively raise their kids.

Even though I am the leader of our home, I can't imagine leading my family without my wife. Without her, leading and raising our children would be impossible. She is the boots-on-the-ground intelligence that brings me "up to speed" with what is going on with our kids.

So I change diapers. I have tea parties with my girls. My wife takes the lead in Bible reading and prayer before bedtime when I am away. But duties like this fall within the context of the roles God has given us—and we improvise, whenever necessary, in order to faithfully fulfill them in our particular home.

BEING DIFFERENT WHILE BEING THE SAME

Every couple will fulfill their roles differently, but all couples are following the same pattern: that of Christ and the church. Even Sean and I have different styles, which have worked themselves out as we've married our wives, had children, and entered into the different seasons of our marriages and families. He might set up some details at his home or in his marriage differently from how I do. Details differ, but our roles do not. Both he and I can encourage each other to fulfill the husband and father roles that God has revealed to us and has called us to fulfill. The same is true for every wife and mother who is seeking to honor God in her roles.

So be different from other marriages while staying the same. As we all seek this, the same pattern will emerge across our marriages: Christ and his church.

Until then,
Spencer and Taylor

DISCUSSION QUESTIONS

1. Do you believe that the way in which your marriage and family function is helping you in or hindering you from fulfilling your God-given role?

2. Are there any ways you wish your spouse would help around the house, with the family, or in the area of work? What are they?

3. Take time to write down one home or family whose family rhythm you admire as your spouse, separately, does the same. Then come together to compare notes and explain why you each admire the home or family you have picked.

CULTIVATING A
SPIRITUAL MARRIAGE

Sean

Dear Romantic,

You and your spouse will develop habits as a married couple that impact you spiritually in one way or the other. Some habits may be good and some may be bad, but they will make a difference all the same.

In fact, you have habits right now you that you might not even realize. It could be that you are in the habit of praying before every meal. Maybe that is the only time you pray. Maybe you are in the habit of going to church on Sundays. Or maybe you always set the alarm but predictably sleep in during the service time. Perhaps you read the Bible before work in the morning or listen to a devotional when you commute. Or maybe you read it before bed. Or maybe the days and nights always seem to get the best of you, and you continually lose track of time.

During the first years of marriage, your habits can chart the course of your next thirty or sixty years as a couple. It is like aiming a bow and arrow—wherever you aim it, the arrow will fly. Turning the bow one inch now might not seem like a big deal, but that one inch has an impact on the arrow's trajectory for hundreds of feet once it flies through the air.

In order to have a spiritual marriage, you must have good spiritual habits. Some of these will be formal and some will be informal, and both will be formed through discipline and intentionality.

FORMAL SPIRITUAL HABITS

Formal spiritual habits have a planned beginning, middle, and end. They are events that happen on a regular basis—events that are expected and anticipated. There is a block of time scheduled on the calendar along with an agenda for habits like this.

Before you start to sweat and skip this letter, let me say that this isn't complicated. The hard part isn't knowing what to do; it is actually doing it. The softball is on the tee for you. You just have to swing.

The formal habits you must cultivate as a married couple are pondering Scripture, praying to God, and praising him through singing.

Pondering the Bible together (see Ps. 1:1–6; Col. 3:16). Reading the Scriptures together is like opening a window when you're in a stuffy house. Hearing from God as he speaks through his Word refreshes the senses and clears away sin and unbiblical thinking.

Pondering the Bible should be a daily event for you as a couple. Pondering simply means thinking upon the law of the Lord and discussing how to apply it to your lives. This could look like reading together in the morning before work or in the evening right before the lights go out. You could read the Bible separately and then discuss it at a designated time each day. You could listen to the Bible while you drive to work and then call your spouse on your lunch break. You could go through one verse or one chapter as a family at dinnertime. All those options are legitimate. What matters isn't primarily how much you read, or when you do it, but the fact that you are pondering the Bible together. Don't just read so that you get through the material and check off a box. Read so that you remember and recall throughout the day.

Praying together (see Eph. 6:18; Col. 4:2; James 5:16). Praying together is a reminder to you as a couple that you are not God and that you need his help. It teaches you not to fear but to cast all your cares upon him. It is the way in which God will advance his kingdom through your family—when you pray, you invite his kingdom to come and his will to be done in your lives (see Matt. 6:10).

Praying together as a couple should be a daily event. You can pray together for five minutes or for fifty minutes. These prayers can take place in the kitchen, in the car, or on the patio. The issue isn't how long or where you pray but that you pray as a couple. Praying together gives you both an opportunity to hear about each other's needs and struggles and then to lay them at the feet of Jesus.

Praising God together in song (see Eph. 5:19; Col. 3:16). Singing together (yes, out-loud singing) is a humbling activity that softens hard hearts. Praising God together will stir your affections for Jesus. It will help you to build each other up in the faith.

My wife Jenny is a phenomenal singer. I have the musical

capability of a chalkboard. It is humbling to initiate a song if you are bad at singing. But the Bible doesn't say, "Only those couples who qualify for a nationally broadcasted competition should sing to each other songs, hymns, and spiritual songs." Instead it says we are to be "addressing one another in psalms and hymns and spiritual songs, singing and making melody to the Lord with your heart" (Eph. 5:19).

It doesn't really matter what kinds of songs you sing. You can sing from the *Trinity Psalter*, the *Baptist Hymnal*, or Andrew Peterson's or the Gettys' latest album. It doesn't matter if you sing for ten minutes or for one minute. You can sing all four verses of "Be Thou My Vision" or just sing one question from *Songs from the New City Catechism*.

It doesn't matter if you sing after a meal (see Mark 14:26) or right before bed (see Ps. 77:6). What matters is that you take courage and sing in a way that changes you. When you sing in faith and with thanksgiving, be prepared to watch the melody melt all ice from your heart and soothe any trouble in your soul.

INFORMAL SPIRITUAL HABITS

We have talked about the formal habits of worship that you should cultivate as a couple, but there are informal habits as well. These informal habits are found in Deuteronomy 6:6–7.

And these words that I command you today shall be on your heart. You shall teach them diligently to your children, and shall talk of them when you sit in your house, and when you walk by the way, and when you lie down, and when you rise.

God wanted the people of Israel to learn his commands and to talk about them diligently throughout the day.

Talking about them "diligently" requires intentionality. "Throughout the day" means informally. God wants his Word to be the topic of conversation when families are sitting in the living room, walking to the mailbox, lying down to sleep, and brushing their teeth in the morning.

Is the Bible intentionally infused into your normal routines? Do you discuss it with your spouse?

The formal habits that we covered above can serve as a great framework for cultivating informal spiritual habits in your marriage.

Ponder and discuss the Bible (Heb. 3:13). Jenny and I typically plan to read through the Bible in a year. We each try to keep our daily Bible reading on the same passage of Scripture so that we can readily discuss it and be familiar with the same story and passage each day.

Typically, when we are brushing our teeth, I will ask Jenny, "Did you read anything that stuck out to you today?" or "Did you learn anything new today from your Bible reading?" I cannot tell you how much I have learned from listening to Jenny share the insights she has received from her time reading and meditating on the Bible. In fact, what she says will often stick with me longer than my own reading reflections do.

Pray without ceasing (1 Thess. 5:17). Praying informally is a habit that will draw you nearer to God, and there are countless opportunities for you to do so. Perhaps you get a phone call from a relative that brings bad news. Once you hang up the phone, you can look at your spouse and say, "That was troubling. Let's take a brief moment to pray for them."

Jenny and I have a habit of pausing and praying in the car when we see an emergency vehicle go by with its lights on. We figure that we will want someone praying for us if an ambulance ever takes one of us to the hospital.

Whether we are praying together spontaneously in a stressful moment, praying for wisdom before discussing a decision, or thanking God immediately for answering prayer, informal prayer continues to remind us that we are not God. We are not God, and we need him.

Praise God through song (Ps. 100:3–4). Singing informally is one of the most pleasant of all habits. Jenny humming "Before the Throne of God Above" while doing dishes is more beautiful than the singing of birds on a spring day. Watching our son Chandler dance to a catechism song from my phone will bring me a deep smile no matter what is going on. Hearts that are happy in God can't help but overflow. Out of the abundance of the heart, the home sings.

These informal habits are perhaps the most enjoyable, because they seem fresh and spontaneous. And yet they aren't random. They are intentional and strategic. It takes intentionality to ask a simple question about the Bible while driving to the grocery store. It takes thoughtfulness to pause and pray for thirty seconds with your spouse when the need arises. It takes strategic planning and discipline not to click "next" on one more episode and instead to save time so that you won't have to rush through "pondering, praying, and praising."

All the decisions you make to cultivate these informal habits will develop a culture of spiritual health and holiness in your home. These unseen habits add up and leave a significant impact on your marriage for decades. Small choices turn into lifestyles that will eventually produce either a bountiful harvest or a hollow regret.

Don't be ashamed and paralyzed if you haven't started any spiritual habits yet. You can start today and invest into forever.

Until then,
Sean

DISCUSSION QUESTIONS

1. Are there any formal habits you currently have that you want to deepen or develop more?
2. Which of the formal habits do you feel the most comfortable with? Why?
3. Which of the formal habits do you feel the least comfortable with? Why?
4. What bad informal habits do you currently have? What good informal habits do you need to intentionally cultivate?
5. When was the last time a passage (or verse) of Scripture stayed in your mind throughout the day? What was it?

SUFFERING IN MARRIAGE

Spencer

Dear Romantic,

We had just celebrated our second anniversary a few days earlier. We put our daughter to bed after our evening prayer meeting at church, sat down, and began debriefing our day. Then the call came. My mom was hysterical. "Dad is unconscious. He's going to the hospital. Get here fast." We packed our car as quickly as we could and started our drive. We got the call before we got out of our city—Dad had died.

One month later, my second daughter was born. After we came home, Taylor couldn't shake overwhelming feelings of sadness. Our doctors told us that women commonly struggle with postpartum depression after giving birth, but we didn't expect it to last as long as it did. The dark days extended their shadows throughout the year. My wife and I would sit in our living room, asking questions that we didn't know how to answer and trying to align the promises of God's Word with the suffering we were experiencing in our lives.

Maybe you have already suffered deeply during these first

years. Maybe you have been given a joyful season at the outset of your marriage. Regardless of what the Lord has given you, his Word tells you that suffering will mark your life and marriage (see Acts 14:21–22; Rom. 8:17; 1 Peter 4:12).

Even though we might know to expect suffering in our lives, we are rarely *ready* for it. But I want you to know that God is— and his Word offers you the two things that you need when suffering arises: compassion and comfort.

GOD HAS COMPASSION FOR YOUR SUFFERING

Suffering will expose what you *need*. When we suffer, our reflex is to find someone or something that can give us the help we need for the pain, the tragedy, the shock, the trauma we are experiencing. We want to know that we aren't alone and that there are resources available to help us to get to the other side of suffering in one piece. Does anyone have compassion for the type of suffering we are going through?

God does.

God knows about your suffering, and he promises to give you his compassion.

> As a father shows compassion to his children,
> so the LORD shows compassion to those who fear him.
> For he knows our frame;
> he remembers that we are dust. (Ps. 103:13–14)

God does not look at us with spite or with a hard heart, wishing that we would pull it together. Instead, he's like a father who is looking at his children with compassion. God knows our weaknesses. He knows that we are made of dust. He wants us to take our burdens and entrust them to his care (see 1 Peter 5:6–7).

God also gives you words for when you are suffering. He has provided words for you when suffering surrounds you and you feel like your heart is failing (see Ps. 40:12). He provides words for you to pray to him when you feel like he has abandoned you (see Ps. 13). He has provided words for you when it seems like everything has been taken from you (see Ps. 73:25–26). Take the words that God has given you in Scripture and pray them back to him. Let his living Word shape your thoughts and prayers as you process your suffering.

Even when your suffering is too deep for words, God compassionately promises to give you exactly what you need through his Spirit (see Rom. 8:26). No matter how deep your suffering is—whether or not it can even be expressed in words—you do not have to run outside God's Word to find what you need.

As you entrust your suffering to him, he promises to give you comfort.

GOD HAS COMFORT FOR YOU
IN YOUR SUFFERING

The reason I want you to process your suffering through the Bible is that Jesus has comfort for any storm that may befall your life and marriage—comfort that only he can provide.

Jesus is the only one who can promise us that incomprehensible suffering means something. How do we process infertility, a miscarriage, the loss of a parent, chronic sickness that medicine doesn't heal, the loss of a job? Only Jesus promises that the affliction we experience is preparing us for glory that will be revealed to us (see 2 Cor. 4:17–18). Only Jesus can say that he is going to make all the crooked things in our lives work together for our good and not for harm (see Rom. 8:28–30). Only Jesus can have the audacity to tell us to rejoice in our sufferings because he is making our faith steadfast (see James 1:2–4). These are deep promises that provide comfort—comfort that only Jesus can give to us when we receive him by faith.

Unlike any other friend, Jesus has perfect knowledge of your suffering: "We do not have a high priest who is unable to sympathize with our weaknesses, but one who in every respect has been tempted as we are, yet without sin. Let us then with confidence draw near to the throne of grace, that we may receive mercy and find grace to help in time of need" (Heb. 4:15–16). Our Savior offers comfort that is tailor-made to the soul of every sufferer, because he has been tempted in *every respect* and has endured it perfectly. He wants you to draw near to him and find exactly what you need.

MODELING GOD'S HEART IN YOUR SUFFERING

Maybe you're not in a specific season of suffering, but your spouse is. How do you faithfully walk beside your spouse as they walk through this valley? God calls you to model his heart for your spouse.

Maybe your spouse has been diagnosed with an illness that changes what you expected your marriage would be like. God calls you to fight the common temptation to become bitter and discontent. He wants you to model his compassion and remember your spouse's frame (see Ps. 103:14) so that you cultivate a heart of tenderness (see 1 Peter 3:8). Remember God's own compassionate heart and extend that same compassion toward your husband or wife (see Ps. 103:13; Col. 3:12).

Maybe your spouse has lost their job, and every door is closing as they search for something new. Money is tight, and they don't understand why God won't answer their prayers. God is calling you to fight against frustration with or dismissal of their trial and instead to encourage them to entrust themselves to him and continue doing good (see 1 Peter 4:19).

God promises to draw near to the brokenhearted (see Ps. 34:18). He has already demonstrated his commitment to do this by drawing near to us through Jesus Christ. Jesus himself was broken, on the cross, so that every broken person can freely enter into God's presence through faith in his blood. Jesus was broken so that those of us who have been broken may be healed (see Isa. 53:5). Bring your suffering to him—and receive the comfort that only he can provide.

Until then,
Spencer

DISCUSSION QUESTIONS

1. What do you think you need when you are suffering?
2. Are there any doubts you have about God's ability to provide what you need in your season of suffering? What are they?
3. In what ways is it difficult for you to model God's heart for your spouse when they are suffering?
4. Are there any particular truths about God's character that bring you comfort or give you ways to understand your suffering?

DOUBTING GOD

Spencer

Dear Romantic,

Your zeal has run dry. The faith you have known all your life is now your greatest source of suspicion. The assurance you once had now feels like a twig in a hurricane of doubt. Where is God? Who is Jesus? What is the Bible? Do you really believe any of it? Just asking the questions makes your heart sink. On top of that, you look out to the world, and the life that others are living looks just fine. Would it be easier to just walk away? What impact would that have on your life? What would it do to your spouse?

Or maybe you are that spouse. That faith you admired in your husband or wife, which was once so clear and true, is now covered by the black fog of doubt. You sit on the couch and lovingly listen, but some of the things that you hear your spouse say frighten you. How can your marriage portray the gospel if your spouse doubts that very gospel? What should you do?

Dealing with doubt, or caring for someone who is in the middle of it, is a complex experience that will be unique to every person. As you seek to walk through this valley together with your spouse, it's important for you to know the common causes of doubt. This will help both of you hold fast to the anchor of Scripture in the middle of the winds and waves that feel like they may destroy your faith or the faith of one you love.

THE WAVES OF SUFFERING

In times of suffering, we think, "God, this is hard. Help me know that you're there." And persistent suffering compounds our doubts. "Help me know that you're there" snowballs into "God, are you there?"—which over time morphs into "God, where are you?!" This happens when the promises that we find in God's Word don't seem to align with what we find in our lives. Satan himself highlights this and seeks to destroy our faith when we are suffering. We are warned about this exact tactic in Scripture: "Be sober-minded; be watchful. Your adversary the devil prowls around like a roaring lion, seeking someone to devour" (1 Peter 5:8).

Whether it is you or your spouse who is doubting, it's critical for you to recognize that suffering is a regular battleground for doubt. Peter specifically tells us that Satan himself "prowls around like a roaring lion" and seeks "someone to devour." So how do you respond to a lion?

You stand firm.

Resist him, firm in your faith, knowing that the same kinds of suffering are being experienced by your brotherhood throughout the world. And after you have suffered a little while, the God of all grace, who has called you to his eternal glory in Christ, will himself restore, confirm, strengthen, and establish you. (1 Peter 5:9–10)

God wants you to fortify your faith. This happens when you recognize the spiritual realities that are at play in your doubt. Recognize that Satan wants to destroy your faith—and that God himself promises to restore you, confirm you, strengthen you, and establish you. We are called to turn on the light of Scripture when we are in the dark room of doubt—to recognize that we aren't wrestling against flesh and blood (see Eph. 6:12). This truth gives those who are seeking to respond to the doubts of their spouses something to say. You can encourage your spouse to resist Satan by trusting in God's promises. Read 1 Peter 5:8–11 together regularly as a way of reminding yourselves of this truth.

THE CLOUDS OF INDIFFERENCE

But what happens when the soul is indifferent to its doubts? What if your spouse has not only grown cold but also isn't as concerned about it as you are? Or what if you are realizing, as you read this, that it describes *you*—even if you hadn't been thinking much about it?

Scripture teaches that we, as believers, must pay close attention to what we hear so that we don't drift away from the faith (see Heb. 2:1) and that we must take great care over our hearts so that we cultivate faith (see Heb. 3:12). The assumption of these passages is that it is possible for Christians to get sleepy. We neglect our Bibles, stifle our prayer lives, and isolate ourselves from other Christians. When David didn't confess his sin, it hindered his relationship with God. His bones dried up (see Ps. 32:3), and he lost strength (see v. 4).

What breaks open our dry hearts when we have been lulled by sin? Nothing but the Word of God. "The law of the LORD is perfect, *reviving the soul*" (Ps. 19:7). When Christians feel the pangs of spiritual malnourishment, they need the food of God's

Word (see Deut. 8:3). This means that you should read the Bible even when you don't feel like it. It means that if you have become disturbed by your lack of spiritual desire, you should throw yourself down by the streams of water that are given to us in Scripture (see Ps. 1).

If you are seeking to care for a spouse who has grown cold to spiritual things, you should seek to provide an environment of truth for them. If they are governing their life by the lies of the world, speak the truth of Scripture to them with gentleness and love. Make your home a greenhouse of God's truth where faith grows.

THE DARKNESS OF DOUBT

Sometimes there is no obvious reason for your doubt. You are not experiencing persistent suffering. You are reading your Bible; you are praying; you are seeking the Lord. Yet your heart still feels overcome with doubt. Feelings of doom and darkness grip you. Or maybe this describes your spouse. How do you help either yourself or your spouse when there are no obvious ways to "fix" the problem?

God's purpose isn't necessarily for you to figure out how to "fix" your problem by focusing all your attention on the dynamics of your doubt. Instead, he's calling you to hope in him. When David did not understand why his soul was cast down and in turmoil, he gave himself this counsel: "Hope in God; for I shall again praise him, my salvation and my God" (Ps. 42:5–6). When Paul reflected on a time when he and others had been "burdened beyond our strength," he didn't obsess over all the causes for why this had happened to them. Instead he said that its purpose had been "to make us rely not on ourselves but on God who raises the dead" (2 Cor. 1:8–9).

Do not fail to recognize that in Scripture we often see God forming us through our burdens before freeing us from our burdens. Although shadows of doubt surround you, God wants you to feel his presence (see Ps. 23:4). So do not draw away from the Lord. Draw near to him. Surround yourself with the saints at your church. Tell them plainly about the season you are in. Spend time with friends and leaders who will remind you of the truths of God's Word.

When your life or your faith is shaken, you will run to where you believe you can find sturdy ground. My prayer for you is that you will run to the only Rock that will guard you when you're in the storm of doubt—whatever the cause of that doubt may be. If you are seeking to love a spouse who is in a season of doubt, then your call is to help to lead them to this Rock that will be their refuge.

> Hear my cry, O God,
>   listen to my prayer;
> from the end of the earth I call to you
>   when my heart is faint.
> Lead me to the rock
>   that is higher than I,
> for you have been my refuge,
>   a strong tower against the enemy. (Ps. 61:1–3)

Until then,
Spencer

DISCUSSION QUESTIONS

1. If you are experiencing doubt, do you notice any relationship between that doubt and any suffering or indifference
that is in your life?
2. Have you created a "greenhouse of God's truth" in your
home? What are some practical ways that you and your
family can do this?
3. Identify another couple in your church who can partner
with you during this season. Be honest with them about
the doubts you are experiencing, and ask them to walk
alongside you.

MONEY, POSSESSIONS, AND GENEROSITY

Sean

Dear Romantic,

Just like the law of thermodynamics or the law of gravity, there is a law of matrimony.

It's a rather simple law: "Stuff piles up."

It is unavoidable—you are going to accumulate things in your marriage. Each year, friends and family will give you all kinds of gifts—from dishes to electronics, towels to trinkets.

Plus, after all the initial showers and parties, you and your spouse will start making your own purchases together. If you're like most, you'll buy new cars, bigger screens, nicer clothes, more toys . . . the list goes on.

And here, I want to shoot a flare into the sky to get your attention. I want to fly a banner over your marriage with giant bold letters that proclaim, "It is more blessed to give than to receive."

JESUS'S PHILOSOPHY

Do we really believe that giving is more blessed than receiving? Most married couples don't live as if Jesus's words in Acts 20:35 are true. We gather rather than give.

The world's philosophy is simple: more things, more thrills. When you have too much stuff, just get a larger house. Build bigger barns and have a better life (see Luke 12:18). You can enjoy life more if you have more. You can kick back and comfort yourself with your ease, security, and entertainment. The world tells you to increase your happiness by gathering.

But Jesus's philosophy is completely the opposite.

We see this first of all when Paul warns us that "those [husbands and wives] who desire to be rich fall into temptation, into a snare, into many senseless and harmful desires that plunge [couples] into ruin and destruction. For the love of money is a root of all kinds of evils. It is through this craving that some [spouses] have wandered away from [their marriages, their families, and God] and pierced themselves [and others] with many pangs" (1 Tim. 6:9–10).

Money isn't the problem—we are. We all have the potential to cling to money more than we cling to Christ. But Jesus said that we cannot serve both God and money, because they are two separate masters (see Matt. 6:24). Whether you save it, spend it, or invest it, money can still infect you with idolatry. God wants you serve him, not money, by saving, spending, and investing it for his glory.

The second place we see Jesus's philosophy on money is when he tells us to increase our happiness by giving.

Since money is a tool that Jesus wants us to use for his glory, and since greed and God's glory don't go together, you and your spouse should give forethought to the way you will use your finances for the church, fellow church members, and strangers.

PRACTICAL PENNIES

How can you begin to give instead of gather? What are some ways you can practice doing so?

Be strategic with money. A great tool for being strategic with your money is a budget—a projection of how you plan to spend your income. I recommend making a budget that tracks your money on at least a monthly basis and sorts it into basic categories. You should sit down together as a couple and chart out how much money you will spend on your home, clothes, groceries, dates, gas, pest control, life insurance, internet, savings, cell phones, retirement, giving, and so on. You can also budget for birthdays, special occasions, and holidays.

At the end of each month, compare your projected spending with your actual spending so you can see where you need to improve and adjust with regard to your goals. There are countless ways that you can track how you spend your money. Early in our marriage, we saved receipts in envelopes. Now we track everything digitally by comparing the charges on our credit cards with the spreadsheet containing our budget.[1]

And, whatever your financial situation, you also need to make sure your budget has a category for giving (see Mark 12:41–44). Plan before the paystub comes. Include a line item for generosity.

1. If you are tempted to overspend and go into debt, credit cards are not for you. However, couples that pay off their credit cards every month can be as "wise as serpents" (Matt. 10:16; see also Luke 16:8) and make a little extra money using credit accounts that allow them to accumulate points and get bonuses.

If you don't plan ahead to be able to give, it will likely not happen (see Prov. 3:9–10). Giving consistently means budgeting money that you can use to bless others. Come together as a couple and start discussing how much you would like to set aside for blessing others. If you don't know where to begin, 10 percent of your income is a great starting point. The Old Testament commonly records people giving this amount of their possessions to others, and we do well to follow it as a baseline for our own giving (see Gen. 14:19–20; 28:20–22).

This process requires you and your spouse to be on the same page and to plan together. If a purchase isn't in your budget, then you must decide together whether to make an exception to the normal way you spend. Talk about it with each other—both of you with an understanding heart and a deferential attitude. Be reasonable with each other (see Phil. 4:5; James 3:17).

It may take time for you to agree on a budget together. Compromises may need to be made and personal preferences crucified. Create your budget with the mindset of Christ Jesus described in Philippians 2:5–8. He was not eager to get his own way, nor was he tied to his heavenly riches. He is the exemplary sacrificial servant whom we are to follow.

If one of you has a different opinion about how much you should give, be gracious to each other. The important thing throughout this process is that you love your spouse and give joyfully. God loves a cheerful giver (see 2 Cor. 9:7). Start by giving at a percentage that will stretch you, and then work backward from there if it isn't possible. You can patiently pray and work toward being able to give that much again.

Be smart with money. Irresponsibility isn't holiness, but frugality isn't righteousness, either. Being smart with your money means carefully treating it as if it isn't yours. We have all made financial choices that essentially lit our money on fire. You could be overspending on internet services each month when a much cheaper option is available. Maybe you have a subscription service that you never actually use and could drop. Maybe you shop at an expensive grocery store when you could find the same products at Walmart. The point is this: find ways to save money.

Why? Because our money belongs to God (see Ps. 24:1; 1 Tim. 6:17–19). Couples are simply stewards. God wants to entrust us with eternal possessions, but first he observes whether we are good at managing earthly possessions (see Luke 16:11–12). If a steward is not keeping track of the flow of the money he's been entrusted with, how can he give a report to the master? We will be held responsible for how we choose to spend our funds.

Be sacrificial with money. Don't neglect the spirit of your budget. You can be just as greedy when you're saving money *on* a budget as you can if you're blowing money because you're *not* on one. Don't neglect generosity every month just because it doesn't fit your budget. Budgets are meant for man, not man for budgets.

Jesus became poor for us so that we might become rich (see 2 Cor. 8:9). He sacrificed everything so that we might receive everything. If we are to be like Jesus, then we need to stretch ourselves and sacrifice as well (see 2 Cor. 8:2).

A friend of mine asked me a helpful question that you can use to evaluate your own sacrificial giving: Is there a difference between your monetary lifestyle and that of unbelieving married couples who have your same level of income?

If you are making thirty thousand dollars a year, your lifestyle shouldn't look the same as a responsible unbeliever's who is bringing in the same amount of cash. If you make three hundred thousand a year, then your lifestyle should look different from that of other married couples who are at that same level. Why? Because unbelievers aren't giving sacrificially to the church. Unbelievers spend their days storing up treasures here on earth. Jesus wants us to store up treasures in heaven.

WHERE SHOULD YOU GIVE?

When you are planning your budget, there are at least three categories of giving that you can consider.

Local Church. The focal point of your giving should be the church that holds your membership. God advances his kingdom through his church, and I've never found a biblical reason to give another ministry precedence over it. The Bible assumes that Christians will be supporting their local churches (see Acts 2:45; 4:32–35; 1 Tim. 5:17–18).

You should set aside a portion of your income to give to your church—no matter what. Regardless of how you think the pastors should spend the money, give. Whether or not you like the way it is being spent, give. Until you move your membership, don't move your money. Don't vote for your preferences with your pocket. We are not called to supervise the books; we are called to obey the Book.

Local Care. In addition to giving to your church, giving to local needs that you see among your family and friends will bring you joy as well (see Gal. 6:10). Contemplate setting aside a small amount that you can designate as a "local care" or "local ministry" fund. This could be used to provide a meal for a new mom or someone in the hospital. We often use ours to replenish our tract supply or to buy a tin of tea to mail to a family we love.

Global Causes. Along with meeting needs close to you that you can see directly, you can also be involved in good that's being done in faraway places, by donating money to global causes. One idea for how to do this is to pick a handful of special ministries that you can donate to during particular months of the year. You can eagerly look forward to giving to pro-life organizations in January. Or in February you could plan to donate to, and pray for, causes that fight human trafficking. March could be the month your whole family supports foster care. December could be the season for a specific focus on world missions. Make a big deal out of these months. It can help your joy to increase when you are able to choose each organization as a couple and partner together for the glory of God. And get your kids involved, even when they are at a very early age! Think about how to involve their hearts and minds in this giving, even though the money is coming from your wallet.

Not every couple can give in these ways during every season. Some seasons might require you to trim your giving in order to provide for your own household. We don't want to fail to provide for our families and thus be deemed worse than unbelievers (see 1 Tim. 5:8). Difficult seasons when we can't give as much as we'd like to are times for us to trust the Lord in a unique way.

God gives possessions to couples so they can use them to bless his people. He gives us money so that we can advance his kingdom. He gives us earthly success so that we can bless God himself and richly enjoy his gifts (see Eccl. 9:8).

God cares about our money, because he cares about our hearts (see Matt. 6:21). If you throw your budget together hastily or carelessly, that is a heart issue. If you make it in a defensive way, such as planning to horde or save because you are scared, that is a heart issue. If you are unwilling to spend money on nice gifts for your spouse, it is a heart issue. If you can't enjoy nice things and be thankful for them, it is a heart issue (see 1 Tim. 6:17). If you are reckless with your budget, it is a heart issue. God doesn't want scrooges who save every penny, nor does he want you to throw money around without thought. Jesus wants you to give freely, fully, and without guilt.

Have you experienced the blessedness that comes from giving instead of gathering?

Until then,
Sean

DISCUSSION QUESTIONS

1. What are the specific priorities should you have in view when making your budget (giving, saving, splurging, paying off debt, and so on)? Are there any areas of your budget on which you and your spouse have different perspectives?
2. Do you get more joy from giving or from getting?
3. Do you feel guilty for enjoying the perks that wealth brings? Or are you able to be thankful for them?
4. Does your lifestyle match the same standard of living that unbelievers have?
5. When was the last time you felt the pain of sacrificial giving?

LEISURE AND ENTERTAINMENT

Spencer

Dear Romantic,

It's finally Friday, and there's nothing on the calendar.

It's been about a month since you've had a good date night. Between your jobs, your church, and visits from your family, it seems like you haven't been able to relax, rest, and have fun together for some time. It's time for some good old-fashioned R & R. It's time to refresh.

So, what do you do?

"Come on!" you say. "Do we really need advice on how to relax?!" Maybe not. But there are two reasons it's important for you to reflect on this topic during the first years of your marriage.

You encounter serious temptations every time you rest. Our culture is an entertainment culture. A host of entertainment platforms offer countless ways for us to entertain ourselves. What should we watch? What should we laugh at? How much time should we spend on entertainment? God calls us to be wise and thoughtful in our Christian lives because we live in evil days (see Eph. 5:15–16), and he calls us to guard ourselves against worldliness (see 1 John 2:15–17). How do you enjoy entertainment that is produced by the world without being worldly yourself? Is that even possible?

God thinks that rest is important. God thought that it was important to give his people specific instructions regarding how to rest (see Ex. 31:12–17). Solomon thought that it was important to tell us to enjoy our lives (see Eccl. 2:24–26). Even Jesus took his disciples on a retreat so that they could rest (see Mark 6:31–32). Indeed, whether we eat or drink or whatever we do, we are called to do it to the glory of God (see 1 Cor. 10:31)—and this includes how we spend our time as we rest.

So how can you enjoy your evening, your date night, your weekend, your vacation, or simply your life in a way that glorifies God and honors his design?[1]

REST IS A RHYTHM, NOT A REFUGE

I know the feeling: It's been a long Monday. You're in the last hour of work. You're stressed. You're burdened. Maybe you're anxious. And your mind drifts toward home. You sigh and say under your breath, "I just need a veg night." You zone out with a night of takeout and TV with your spouse. Then Tuesday comes, and the burdens and anxiety are back. Your mind drifts home and back to the same serene scene from last night: forgetting your troubles over a show and a bowl of ice cream. You think to yourself, "I just need a veg night." And you repeat this pattern all week.

---

1. If you want to dig deeper into how you can enjoy God by enjoying his gifts in this world, check out Joe Rigney, *The Things of Earth: Treasuring God by Enjoying His Gifts* (Wheaton, IL: Crossway, 2015).

The problem with this picture is not the particulars, such as TV or ice cream. The problem with it is that it takes an expression of rest and turns it into refuge for your soul. The TV—or a book, or food, or exercise, or a hike, or a nap, or any other good thing that God has made—calls out to us and says, "Come and veg. Give me your burdens and stress, and I'll help you to *forget*" . . . but Jesus calls out to us with a different call: "Come to me, all who labor and are heavy laden, and I will give you *rest*" (Matt. 11:28).

When we are burdened and weary, we are tempted to treat entertainment, vacations, movies, and restaurants as refuges. But instead God has designed rest and entertainment to help us to remember that he is our only refuge (see Ps. 46:11). Resting means ceasing our regular activity and doing something that reminds us that we are not God. We can do this in a thousand different ways—including movie nights with our spouses over a bowl of ice cream. But instead of consisting of "veg nights" that we hope will take all our burdens away, rest is to be a rhythm that helps us to remember the God who carries our burdens when we cast them on him (see 1 Peter 5:7).

REST IS A GIFT, NOT A GIVEN

When God is our refuge, we see rest as a gift from him and not a given that we assume and demand. Some of the most surprising conflicts my wife and I have had in our first years of marriage have come about as a result of talking about how we both want to rest.

"Let's go on a walk tonight!" is answered with "Why don't we play a board game instead?"

"Do you want to watch a movie?" collides with "Can we have a quiet night reading?"

"Let's catch up and talk tonight" is met by "I was hoping to play video games."

When we believe that rest is our refuge, then we believe that we *must have it*. We expect rest. We see it as a given and want to spend our free time on our own desires—and we want our spouses to get on board. These desires clash, and a battle can erupt. This is exactly what Scripture tells us to expect—that when our desires are at war within us, they lead us to fight (see James 4:1).

But God wants us to see that the rest we get is a gift that we receive from him (see James 1:17)—not something that we demand or expect. This means that we can receive all types of rest as being good—even those that we don't prefer—because everything that God has made is good and should be received with thanksgiving, and is even made holy through prayer (see 1 Tim. 4:4–5).

God, not our nightly jog, is our refuge. God, not our favorite show, is our rest. God, not video games, carries our burdens. So we can surrender our own way, and our demands and preferences (see 1 Cor. 13:4–5; Phil. 2:3–4), and can use entertainment and leisure as a means of serving our spouses—and can also receive whatever rest God gives us as a gift from him.

REST IS EARTHY, NOT WORLDLY

Although God doesn't want your rest to be worldly, he does want it to be earthy.

God has made a world that contains evening walks, friends, sports, chocolate cake, sex, bookstores, movies, beach vacations, pumpkin patches, baseball, and a thousand other created things that can refresh us and remind us of him. This created world can be a bane to our spiritual growth, but it can also be a boon to it;

and this happens when every gift that we receive leads to praise and thanksgiving to him.

When we participate in earthy rest, we can discover wonderful opportunities. For example, you might find that your non-Christian neighbor loves the same sports team that you do. You can invite him over to watch the game with you at your house and can build a relationship with him that provides you a chance to share the gospel. Or earthy rest might provide opportunities for you to deepen your relationship with another Christian couple. My wife and I got close to some of our best friends when we found out that we all enjoyed the same TV show and started watching it together once a week. We enjoyed mutual encouragement as we got together each week and talked before and after the program.

But as we enjoy earthy rest, we also avoid worldly rest. Although Scripture teaches that this created world is good (see 1 Tim. 4:4), it also teaches that it is broken and deeply influenced by sin and by Satan (see 1 John 5:19). We must hold both of these truths in our hearts as we rest. God calls us to holiness—to be those who don't have sexual immorality, impurity, or covetousness even named among us, and who avoid crude joking (see Eph. 5:3–4). It's not legalistic for us to refuse to watch certain shows or movies or to avoid certain places or activities that we know will lead us to sin. Such refusal comes not from a heart of legalism but from a heart of love for Jesus that motivates us to say no to the things of this world in order that we may know and experience more of him.

So, here's to your evening, your weekend, your vacation, and your marriage. Enjoy and receive these gifts for what they are: opportunities for you to remember God, enjoy his gifts, and worship him in the world he has made.

Until then,
Spencer

DISCUSSION QUESTIONS

1. Do you find it easy, or hard, to rest? Why?
2. What forms of rest are you most tempted to seek refuge in?
3. Ask your spouse what refreshes them the most. Why?
4. What could you do to sacrifice your own preferences in order to help your spouse to be refreshed more regularly?

OPENING YOUR HOME

Spencer

Dear Romantic,

There is a habit that is essential for you to cultivate in the first years of your marriage.

If you cultivate this habit, you and your spouse will be given surprising opportunities to grow. You will encounter opportunities to do frontline gospel ministry together. You will grow in your faith and help others to grow in their faith. You will help the hurting. You will have fun. You will laugh. You will cry. You will grow closer to each other and to other people. You may make friendships that will last a lifetime.

I'm talking about the habit of hospitality.

Some of the most important moments in your marriage won't happen on vacation. They won't happen on a marriage retreat. They won't happen on a perfectly orchestrated date night. They will happen on your couch, over a bowl of ice cream, as you share your home with others—both those whom you know and those whom you don't know.

During these first years of marriage, you have a freedom that many other married couples don't have. Your new family has just begun, and your habits are still in the process of taking shape. Right now is the time when you are making the habits that you will be living with forty years from now. My hope is that you will cultivate the habit of hospitality.

Let me tell you why.

HOSPITALITY IS URGENT

One of the primary ways that God wants to care for suffering Christians is through our homes.

> The end of all things is at hand; therefore be self-controlled and sober-minded for the sake of your prayers. Above all, keep loving one another earnestly, since love covers a multitude of sins. Show hospitality to one another without grumbling. (1 Peter 4:7–9)

The "end of all things" that Peter is referring to is the entire time before Jesus returns. This time is marked by suffering and difficulty for believers. We will be tempted to give up hope and not to endure until the end. So what will God provide to aid believers with keeping their faith until the end?

Our couches. Our dinner tables. Our guest bedrooms.

Peter says that the end is near. And this leads him to give the command "Show hospitality to one another without grumbling." God wants you to think about your home as being ground zero for evangelism and discipleship in a hostile world. It's one of the primary hubs of the church's spiritual activity in the time before Jesus returns. Hospitality is urgent.

HOSPITALITY IS HARD

Hospitality doesn't naturally happen. You have to seek out opportunities to be hospitable (see Rom. 12:13). You must be proactive—must make yourself vulnerable to awkward situations and serve other people without expecting them to serve you in return.

A regular refrain throughout the Bible is that believers' homes are to be open to the church—a refrain that comes in the form of regular encouragement from various biblical authors (see Acts 2:46; Rom. 12:13). Why do they emphasize this? Because it's so easy for us to neglect it. This is why the author of Hebrews has to encourage us not to "neglect to show hospitality to strangers" by pointing out that "thereby some have entertained angels unawares" (see Heb. 13:2).

The author wants us to think here of Genesis 18, when Abraham showed hospitality to three visitors who were angels—and he *didn't know*. These angels reminded Abraham of the promises God had made to him. The author of Hebrews wants us to know that even though hospitality can be hard, it holds untold and even unexpected blessings.

We need this encouragement, because hospitality isn't "normal." "Normal" is coming home from work, eating dinner, turning on the TV, and relaxing. Hospitality is expensive (your grocery bill will go up!), time-consuming, and energy-draining. It will be easy for you to neglect this during your first years of marriage. Hospitality is hard.

And the *work* of hospitality may not even be the hardest part. The hardest part may be that it will be aimed at strangers. The literal meaning of the Greek word that we translate as *hospitality* is "stranger love." Distinctly Christian hospitality is aimed at those whom we do not know. We are called to invite neighbors, strangers, missionaries, and guests at our church to eat spaghetti at our tables and do family devotions with us before our kids' bedtime.

This will be hard. It might be awkward. And you might not want to do it. . . . Which is why God's Word encourages us so specifically to practice it.

HOSPITALITY IS FOR EVERYONE

"But," you say, "how can we show hospitality?" You want your home and marriage to be places where ministry happens, but perhaps you feel that your circumstances are unique. What if you don't have a big enough house, or both of you work full-time jobs, or you're shy? The good news is that hospitality is about your heart and can fit into any apartment size or type of schedule. Let me show you how.

"We don't have a big enough or nice enough space." Most of us think hospitality requires a clean house, a prepared meal, and bathrooms that have the faint smell of floral air freshener. There is nothing wrong with preparing your home if it helps you to serve people. But if the point of doing so is for other people to admire your home, then such "hospitality" is not about other people anymore.

The point of hospitality is to use our relationships with the saints to refresh them (see Philem. 4–7). You can do that around a beautiful table with a thoughtful meal or on the floor over boxes of Chinese food. Focus on people over appearances.

"We don't have enough time." Maybe you and your spouse are cobbling together several different part-time jobs in order to make marriage work. You barely have time for each other, let alone enough time to set aside for hospitality. But hospitality is

not calling you to somehow add more time to your schedule. Hospitality involves welcoming others into your life, not adding an extracurricular to an already busy life.

Of course, it's wise for you and your spouse to have times of rest for just the two of you. But consider some opportunities you may already have for including other people in your family rhythm. One way might be a family dinner. But this could also include exercising with people in your neighborhood, carpooling with coworkers, grocery shopping with neighbors, or watching the game with a couple from church instead of by yourselves. Hospitality is about being generous with the time that you do have.

An important thing to say to young parents, or to those who are sick, is that God is compassionate. He knows the season you are in. He is not calling you to show the same type of hospitality as people can who have no children or health problems. Instead, he's calling you to be faithful with what you have been given (see Matt. 25:14–30).

"We're shy, and this makes us nervous." God wants to use your personality and your gifts—whatever they are—to bless other people. He has not said that only those who are extroverted should practice hospitality. Instead, he has revealed to all his people that they should "seek to show hospitality" (Rom. 12:13). Introverts have the unique ability to befriend people who feel intimidated by the more bombastic personalities in the church. Maybe this means that you focus on showing hospitality to just one couple in your church over a period of time. Maybe it means walking, in faith, over to your neighbor and introducing yourself.

However hospitality works itself out practically in their situation, every believing couple should ask themselves, "Are we *seeking* to show hospitality in our daily lives?"

We must ask ourselves this question, because so much is at stake.

THE PICTURE OF HOSPITALITY

What, exactly, is at stake? The habit of hospitality is so crucial within your first years of marriage because it can become one of the primary ways that you portray the gospel as a family: "Welcome one another as Christ has welcomed you, for the glory of God" (Rom. 15:7).

The habit of hospitality must arise from our hearts' response to the hospitality that God himself has shown us. When we were at our most stubborn, selfish, and sinful, Jesus welcomed us into God's family through his death and resurrection. We locked ourselves out of God's family—and yet Jesus unlocked the door of heaven, was punished for our sin, and clothed us in his righteousness so that we could boldly enter God's presence and sit at his table.

We will welcome strangers, neighbors, and friends into our homes only when we are motivated by the eternal welcome of God that we ourselves have received in Christ. And when our hearts are motivated by this hospitality that we have received, the hospitality that we extend—whether in the form of a formal meal or last-minute takeout—will be a picture of the gospel itself.

Until then,
Spencer

DISCUSSION QUESTIONS

1. Who is someone who exemplifies hospitality to you? Why?
2. What part of hospitality feels particularly difficult for you?
3. What is one part of your life that you could include another person in?

LOVING YOUR PARENTS

Spencer

Dear Romantic,

Within the first five years of marriage, you will have conversations with your parents in which they will say at least one of the following sentences:

"Have you decided what you will do for the holidays this year?"

"You know, when we first got married . . ."

"Were you planning on talking to us about this decision?"

"Do you need any money?"

Your relationship with both sets of parents could be good, bad, complicated, or even nonexistent. Whatever the case, the way you approach these relationships will have a significant impact on your marriage and family. Should you and your spouse distance yourselves from your parents? After all, you're married now—they don't have a say in your life anymore, right? Should the two of you talk to your parents about everything? What should you do about holidays? Children and grandchildren? Finances? Decision-making?

FULFILLING YOUR ROLE

Our relationships with our parents adjust during different seasons of our lives. The way you relate to your parents should change as you move from dating to engagement and then to marriage. It will change again if the Lord blesses you with children. It will change as your parents get older and need more help. Your goal should not be to come up with one single approach to your relationship with your parents going forward. Instead, you should let love characterize the relationship throughout every season (see Col. 3:14).

Two mistakes you can make in the early years of your marriage will upset the balance of your relationship with your parents: obsessing over them and neglecting them. Both of these mistakes need to be rectified with love.

You *obsess* over your parents when you believe that their words, preferences, and approval are what govern your marriage. You can't make decisions until you talk to your parents. You are paralyzed by their disapproval. Wives, you get nervous if your husbands make a decision that you know your parents won't like—and you refuse to follow his lead. Husbands, you feel tension when your wives disagree with your moms on a particular topic—and you try to avoid this at all costs.

How do you know whether you are obsessing over your parents and throwing your relationship with them off-balance? If your relationship with them hinders you from fulfilling your God-given roles, you need to adjust it. God has called you into a covenant with your spouse. You have left your parents and become one flesh with your husband or wife (see Gen. 2:24). This means that a husband should ask, "How can I lead my family faithfully?" while a wife should ask, "How can I joyfully follow my husband?" Perhaps God is calling you to take a new job that would require moving away from your parents and hometown. Or perhaps you are considering joining a different church from your parents. Maybe your parents have given you advice, but you believe you should do something different. If your primary objection to making certain decisions is solely "My parents will be upset," then you need to remember the central relational role God has given you.

Loving your parents and faithfully leading, or submitting to, your spouse are not opposites. Loving your parents means being patient and kind with them, communicating with them truthfully (see Eph. 4:15), and serving them (see Phil. 2:3–4). God cares about the posture of your heart toward your parents as you fulfill your role in your marriage.

MAKING A RETURN

You may have read everything above and cheered. "Yes! Leave and cleave! They can't tell us what to do!" You viewed the wedding altar as a finish line in your relationship with your parents. Marriage has provided the freedom you have wanted for a long time. Now you simply manage your relationship with your parents and focus primarily on your new marriage.

But this isn't freedom from your parents; it's *neglecting* them—the second mistake we mentioned above. Taking this posture toward your parents uses legitimate biblical freedoms in a way that dishonors God. God's purpose behind the freedom that he gives us is not so that we can finally get to do what we want. His purpose is for us "through love [to] serve one another" (Gal. 5:13).

God expects newly married couples to continue to honor their parents. For example, Paul instructs grown children to "make some return" to their mothers, if their mothers are widowed and in need of care, because doing so is "pleasing in the sight of God" (1 Tim. 5:4). And Jesus rebukes the Pharisees for neglecting their parents and not honoring them (see Mark 7:9–13).[1]

This means that our parents matter. Scripture repeatedly calls for children to honor their parents—even when they are grown—in the way that they speak about them, interact with them, and include them in the fabric of their lives. As much as it depends on us, we should not treat our relationships with our parents the same way that we treat every other relationship. We should treat our parents with a heightened sense of honor (see Ex. 20:12).

THE NEXT STEP OF FAITHFULNESS

Most of us know what Scripture says on this topic. The issue is how we obey what it says with our particular parents. Maybe you have a broken relationship with your parents and haven't spoken to them in years. Perhaps they just told you they would love to hear from you more. It could be that your parents live far away and are getting sick as they get older. Or maybe you've decided you need to do something different for Christmas this year and you know your decision is going to be unpopular with your parents.

The call of the hour is to understand the situation and take the next step of faithfulness toward your parents. Most situations you will face with your parents can be sorted into three categories.

1. The ideas in this paragraph were influenced by Tim Challies's helpful series of articles called The Commandment We Forgot. The first article can be found at Tim Challies, "The Commandment We Forgot," *Challies* (blog), December 1, 2016, https://www.challies.com/articles/the-commandment -we-forgot/, and we recommend continuing to follow the links on the page to the rest of the series.

First, there will be situations in which *honor is easy*. For instance, if you have a good relationship with your parents and both you and they want to honor the Lord, this is a wonderful blessing. You can honor your parents in these times by including them in your life, asking for their help and advice, and communicating with them about what God is doing throughout your first years of marriage.

Second, there will be situations in which *honor is easy but the practical details are complicated*. For example, if your mother is widowed, lives alone, and has just been diagnosed with a chronic illness, she will need help. Perhaps you feel the desire to honor her and recognize that your next step should be to care for her needs by making a return (see 1 Tim. 5:4), but you need wisdom to know what this will look like in your particular circumstances. It could take the form of having her move in with you, arranging care for her in her own hometown, or at least starting the conversation with her.

Third, there will be situations in which *honor is hard*. This might be the case if you and your spouse have decided to not follow parental advice regarding your career choices, your parenting, where you go to church, or countless other details of your lives. How do you honor your parents while also doing what you believe is best? Or perhaps your relationship with your parents is broken and you haven't spoken with them in years—how do you honor them then? The answer is to take the next step of faithfulness. This could mean reading a book on reconciliation[2] and then making plans to contact your parents so you can talk to them. It might mean sitting down with your parents and

2. See, for instance, Ken Sande with Tom Raabe, *Peacemaking for Families: A Biblical Guide to Managing Conflict in Your Home* (Carol Stream, IL: Tyndale House), 2002, and Ernie Baker, *Help! I'm in a Conflict* (Wapwallopen, PA: Shepherd Press, 2015).

explaining a decision to them that you know they will not like.

What is your next step of faithfulness? Answer that question with a prayerful heart and an open Bible, and then ask Jesus for help with taking that step.

UNDOING THE CURSE

In Romans 1, Paul describes the deep impact that sin has had on the human race. At the end of the chapter, he uses strong words to describe people who do not acknowledge God, as well as the sins that they commit. Surprisingly, right in between describing those who are "inventors of evil" and "foolish," Paul mentions people who are "disobedient to parents" (v. 30).

One of the marks of sin's presence in this world is the breakdown of the relationship between children and their parents—which can be seen both in children who throw fits in the grocery store and in adults who haven't talked to their parents in years. This is the hopeless pattern of our sinful hearts.

But Jesus brings hope through his cross and resurrection. He died and rose again so that you and your parents could walk in "newness of life" (Rom. 6:4). When the peace of Christ rules in your heart (see Col. 3:15), you can extend that peace into every relationship you have, and this gives you the power to bring harmony to your relationship with your parents.

Jesus died so that you could have peace in every season and stage of your relationship with your parents. By his grace, let's display that peace and display his gospel for our parents no matter what stage we are in.

Until then,
Spencer

DISCUSSION QUESTIONS

1. Do you struggle with obsessing over or neglecting your parents?
2. What is your next step of faithfulness toward your parents? Talk about this with your spouse.
3. What is one way you can deepen and cultivate your relationship with your parents? Make a plan with your spouse to do so.

UNDERSTANDING YOUR
DIFFERENCES

Spencer

Dear Romantic,

When your marriage began, the differences that existed between you and your spouse were your greatest advantage. It seemed like there could be no areas of weakness in your marriage, because the two of you perfectly complemented each other. There was symmetry and balance. Like bright stars against a dark sky, your differences made your relationship a beautiful thing to behold. They were differences between allies, not enemies.

But now those same differences feel like a liability. You knew you were different from your spouse, but you didn't realize you were *that* different. Now it seems like the very things that you used to love about each other are your most frequent catalysts of conflict. On top of this, your spouse is constantly changing. He or she is not the same now as when you were first married, and you're wondering what other types of differences you will need to navigate in the years ahead.

You weren't expecting to marry a clone of yourself, but you

also weren't expecting your spouse to be *this* different. Is your situation unique? How can you and your spouse be the people God made you to be when it feels like he also made you the complete opposite of each other?

THE GOODNESS OF DIFFERENCE

God thinks it's good that you are different from your spouse. Difference existed before sin entered the world. In the beginning God created light and dark, heaven and earth, land and sea, and animals that fly and walk and swim and creep. And then, to top it off, he made the crown jewel of his creation—human beings—and he made them *different*: "So God created man in his own image, in the image of God he created him; *male and female* he created them. . . . And God saw everything that he had made, and behold, it was *very good*" (Gen. 1:27, 31). Even before we turn our attention to other types of differences, we see that God has designed every marriage to contain first of all the blessed difference of the spouses' genders, to demonstrate forever the goodness of difference.

Even now that sin has distorted what God has made, he is still committed to bringing different people together. In Jesus Christ, God brings people together from different backgrounds, cultures, languages, and times and makes them into one people (see Eph. 2:11–22; Rev. 7:9). The apostle Paul tells us that every member of Jesus's body is different—and that it needs to be that way (see 1 Cor. 12:14–31).

If you feel disheartened about the differences between you and your spouse, have hope. God loves to take things that don't seem to fit together and then unify them to display his glory—and he wants to do the same in your marriage . . . even if it might be a painful process.

THE PROBLEM OF DIFFERENCE

So differences are good—but what happens when they cause complications in your relationship? What should you do about the differences in personality that have emerged between you and your spouse over these first few years? What if you married into a different culture, with different family traditions? Differences that arise from situations like this can seem particularly difficult, because they aren't matters of sin and righteousness but of preferences and habits. And yet when those differences lead to *problems* between you and your spouse, these problems are rooted not in the mere fact that you are different but in the way that your hearts respond to your differences. How should you respond to the non-sinful differences that arise between you and your spouse?

Remember your shared identity. The world wants you to spend most of your time thinking about the ways you are unique from other people. According to secular thinking, you need to know your Myers-Briggs type, Enneagram type, DISC profile, and love language so that you can understand how *you* operate, how *you* approach problems, and how *you* feel loved. These tests and tools can be a helpful source of general observations about how we're uniquely wired. But God's Word tells us that if we want to navigate our differences in a way that honors him, we need to first start with how we are the same.

Whenever Paul discusses differences between Christians, he always returns to their *sameness.* Though we are many, we are one body in Christ (see Rom. 12:5). We should welcome differences because we have all been welcomed by Christ (see Rom. 15:7). We have different gifts, but we have the same Spirit, the same Lord, the same God who empowers us (see 1 Cor. 12:5–6). We have one body, one Spirit, one Lord, one faith, one baptism (see

Eph. 4:4–6). Peter calls husbands to live with their wives and approach their differences in an understanding way. Why? "They are heirs *with you* of the grace of life" (1 Peter 3:7).

You and your spouse should seek to understand your differences. But that understanding will come after you've taken a deep dive into the ways that you are the *same* as children of your heavenly Father through Christ. We can navigate even the most tangled issues that arise from our differences when we begin with a deep understanding of the identity we share in Christ.

Humbly seek to understand your spouse. Thinking about our shared identity in Christ softens our hearts when we see differences in our spouses. We have entered into God's family through the blood of Christ, who took the form of a servant and suffered in our place. When we believe this, it makes us humble. We "count others more significant than [ourselves]," and we "look . . . to the interests of others" (Phil. 2:3–4). We have a soft heart toward our spouses.

This passage in Philippians assumes that we are going to seek to *understand* what the interests of others are.[1] So when we encounter differences in our marriages, we should seek to *understand our spouses.* This means avoiding quick judgments (see Matt. 7:1–4) and being slow to speak and quick to listen (see James 1:19). For spouses who come from different cultures, this might mean researching each other's culture or asking open-ended questions about why both of you enjoy what you do. It also means that we humbly *listen* to our spouses when they share ways in which we can serve them and understand them.

1. For a great practical resource on this, see the PAUSE principle in Ken Sande with Tom Raabe, "Negotiation," chap. 7 in *Peacemaking for Families: A Biblical Guide to Managing Conflict in Your Home* (Carol Stream, IL: Tyndale House), 2002.

Respond with serving hands. When we understand what our spouses' interests are, we will know how to serve them. In Romans 12, immediately after the apostle Paul talks about the unity and diversity of the church, he gives his readers a short command: "Outdo one another in showing honor" (v. 10).

This is God-ordained one-upmanship. Paul calls on believers who have different cultures, backgrounds, personalities, and preferences to honor one another. Honoring your spouse can mean celebrating their unique gifts, personality, or culture. It can mean taking part in what they enjoy. And, because of the unity you both share through Christ, it definitely means finding practical ways to serve them and appreciate who God made them to be.

The ultimate aim of our marriages is the ultimate aim of the entire Christian life—not to please ourselves but to glorify God and love others. We don't gain the ability to accomplish this goal based on how similar to or different from our spouses we are. We find it in the gospel of Jesus Christ. Only Jesus can empower us to do this, because he is the only one who did it perfectly: "For Christ did not please himself, but as it is written, 'The reproaches of those who reproached you fell on me'" (Rom. 15:3). The One who was perfectly righteous served the ones who were ruined and sinful—we couldn't be any more different from him, and yet he could not have served us any more than he did. May your heart be shaped by his cross as you walk this road together with your spouse.

Until then,
Spencer

DISCUSSION QUESTIONS

1. Do you think differences between spouses are a liability or an advantage? Why?
2. What are some ways that you and your spouse are different from each other?
3. Ask your spouse how you can serve them in a way that honors your differences.

ON CONFLICT

Sean

Dear Romantic,

Every spouse is a sinner. I wish this were not so.

This reality produces tensions that are unavoidable in a marriage (see Rom. 3:23; James 4:1). No matter how holy you are or how much you and your spouse love each other, you will find yourselves in conflict.

Some tensions will be mild miscommunications, while others may be heated disagreements. And some may be loud and intense, while others may be subtle and insidious. I've seen some couples explode like Mount St. Helens. They spew hot, volatile, and unpredictable words. Other couples can gently gurgle out lava like a Hawaiian eruption. Their communication is slow, searing, and constantly burning.

Until all is made new and Jesus returns, we will experience some disharmony in our matrimony.

The question is not whether you will have conflict; the question is what you will do with it. It isn't a matter of *when*; it is a matter of *how*.

FIRE EXTINGUISHERS ARE YOUR FRIEND

When conflicts arise in your marriage, you need to have fire extinguishers nearby. Not down the hall as regulations require them to be in an apartment complex, but in close proximity and easy to access. You need them tucked under the sink of your soul.

As the heat begins to rise in your heart, you need to pull out your fire extinguishers and spray. In Colossians 3, Paul describes at least four extinguishers that you should keep close at hand. These are biblical responses that every couple should make use of when they are facing conflict: grace, humility, patience, and forgiveness.

> Put on then, as God's chosen ones, holy and beloved, compassionate hearts, kindness, humility, meekness, and patience, bearing with one another and, if one has a complaint against another, forgiving each other; as the Lord has forgiven you, so you also must forgive. And above all these put on love, which binds everything together in perfect harmony. And let the peace of Christ rule in your hearts, to which indeed you were called in one body. And be thankful. (Col. 3:12–15)

1. Grace. Most arguments that take place in a marriage are about proving someone wrong. Yes, *proving* it. We want to prove that our idea for the weekend schedule is better. We want to prove that our plan for the kids' school year makes more sense.

How can I pin my spouse against the wall and show them that I'm right? How can I win this debate? How can I force them to bow? I'm right, they're wrong, and I'm going to make that crystal clear. You might not think these exact words, but the sentiment is there.

This approach to conflict emphasizes dominance instead of

graciousness. God tells us to put on "compassionate hearts" and "kindness." These are qualities of grace. It is hard to spar when you are being gracious.

Grace seeks understanding over superiority. It doesn't need to prove someone wrong, because it knows what is right. It doesn't take a posture of control. Gentleness and care are its companions, and harshness is nowhere to be found.

When tensions rise, thoughts like these reflect a gracious heart: How can I care for my wife in this moment of confusion between us? How can I be gentle with my husband during this disagreement? If he is wrong on this matter, how can I help him to better understand my perspective? If she sins against me in anger, how can I serve her instead of escalating the situation?

When the heat of anger and the desire for justice surface in your soul, spray it with grace. "Put on then . . . compassionate hearts [and] kindness."

2. *Humility.* Pride burns down marriages—and the flames of self-exaltation can leave third-degree burns on everyone who is involved. We must fight pride with humility. Only humble people know how to work through conflict, because humble people are willing to admit they are wrong. They know they could be missing information or might have misjudged a decision.

The Bible says to clothe yourself with humility (see 1 Peter 5:5; James 4:6), and this includes whenever you are entering a disagreement. Take a posture that reflects the fact that you might be a finite, imperfect spouse. Because you are.

When you are disagreeing with your spouse, do you think there is a chance you could be wrong about whatever the issue is? Or do you think the problem is that your spouse just hasn't realized all the reasons why your position is the correct one? Do you think that if your wife saw the logic behind your wise decision, she wouldn't be frustrated? That if your husband just understood your reasonable rationale, he wouldn't be so obstinate?

Humble spouses don't go into arguments with guns blazing. Humble spouses are slow to speak and quick to hear (see James 1:19). They don't think of themselves more highly than they ought (see Rom. 12:3).

The worst part about the fire of pride is that it may not give off any heat. You don't have to *feel* prideful to be prideful. Keep the extinguisher of humility handy even when you don't see smoke or feel any flames.

3. Patience. Spray your heart down with patience, because impatience leads to conflict. Impatient people are prideful. Whereas patience involves having the humility to not make demands for the sake of your preferences or timetable, when we demand things on *our* terms we are putting ourselves at the center. We are being prideful. Patience gives the benefit of the doubt to someone else instead of arrogantly assuming that your way is right. The Bible says that a patient person is stronger than a warrior (see Prov. 16:32)—and this strength doesn't come from us. It comes from the fruit of the Spirit and enables us to serve others (see Gal. 5:22).

Which of the following pairs of statements sound more loving and Christlike? Which create an enjoyable atmosphere in your home?

"Would you hurry up? We are going to be late."	"My hands are free. Is there anything I can help to pack up or gather?"
"Hurry up. Spit it out. What are you saying?"	"... [caring silence while giving your spouse time to think] ..."

| "How many times have I told you where that goes? Can't you remember where to put things?" | "I noticed that the plates are in the other cabinet again. I think this location made more sense the last time we talked, but would a different spot be better?" |

Patient people make for the most pleasant spouses in the world. Don't you want to be one? Use this fire extinguisher generously on yourself.

4. Forgiveness. Unresolved conflict can be a low-grade fever in marriage. It is always in the background, hindering, and unpleasant—and often leads us to be bitter, feel resentment, take offense, and replay conversations over and over again in our thoughts. It can't be ignored.

In order to bring healing to your marriage, you must be willing to forgive (Matt. 18:21–22). Forgiveness involves a commitment not to hold your spouse's sin against him or her or ever to bring it up in a way that is condemning or unprofitable.

When your spouse sins against you, you will need to have a heart of forgiveness—but don't wait until the moment of sin to cultivate a forgiving spirit. Have a tender heart *before* sin takes place. Be ready to forgive. Pull out the extinguisher at the first whiff of the smoke of sin and bitterness. Have your finger on the trigger so that you are ready to pour out the foam of forgiveness when the time comes (see Eph. 4:31–32).[1]

---

1. For more details on how and when to forgive someone, see Heath Lambert, *A Theology of Biblical Counseling: The Doctrinal Foundations of Counseling Ministry* (Grand Rapids: Zondervan, 2016), 235–46; Heath Lambert, "Should I Forgive Someone Who's Not Sorry They Sinned?" September 29, 2016, in *Truth in Love*, produced by Association of Certified Biblical Counselors, podcast, mp3 audio, 9:30, https://biblicalcounseling.com/forgive

The only way you can truly forgive is to have a heart that is softened by the good news of Jesus. Meditating on his sacrifice will help you to have a tender heart. If, however, you delay forgiveness, you allow bitterness to take root. Bitterness always grows in our hearts when we neglect the gospel—but it is broken at the foot of the cross, as we think about how Jesus has forgiven us of our innumerable sins (see 1 John 1:9). We must lay hold of his forgiveness by faith in order to be able to extend it to our spouses.

FULL OF LOVE

All four of these fire extinguishers are also filled with love.

When you are in a conflict, the most important thing for you to do is to love God and your spouse.

Love is patient, gracious, and kind. It is humble. It isn't full of envy, boasting, or rudeness. It isn't self-seeking or quickly angered. It always hopes, believes the best, and is ready to forgive. It never fails (see 1 Cor. 13). We must be loving people who are full of grace, humility, patience, and forgiveness.

Keep these four extinguishers close at hand and use them often. They won't run out or expire.

Until then,
Sean

-someone-whos-not-sorry-sinned-transcript/; and Robert D. Jones, appendix A of *Pursuing Peace: A Christian Guide to Handling Our Conflicts* (Wheaton, IL: Crossway, 2012).

DISCUSSION QUESTIONS

1. Is there any conflict currently in your marriage that has not been resolved?
2. Think about the last conflict you had. Which fire extinguisher do you need to have ready in your heart in order to prevent a repeat of that conflict?
3. Does your spouse view you as a gracious, humble, patient, and forgiving person? Ask for their honest opinion as well as for specific examples of ways that you can improve.

HAVE WE FALLEN OUT OF LOVE?

Spencer

Dear Romantic,

Do you remember it?

The way your heart raced when your spouse walked into the room. The surges of happy anxiety. The thrill and the thoughtless abandon that came from being together. Time flew by. Then— marriage. When you and your spouse met at the altar and gave your lives to each other, you knew you were receiving a glorious gift. Your honeymoon—giving your bodies to each other and being intoxicated with love. Those first months of marriage were a joy. You were confident that nothing would steal your love for each other.

But something has happened. Your relationship feels like a sparkler that ignited quickly but has now been burned and spent. It feels useless. You go on dates and try to talk, but nothing catches, so you come home early and turn on the TV because there's nothing else to do. You used to look forward to seeing your spouse every day, but the excitement is gone now. You feel numb. You wish you could say you had the desire to make it work, but if you're honest, it's hard even to want your spouse anymore.

You sit down with a friend and share all of this with them, and they say those words you have been too scared to think: "Do you think you have fallen out of love?"

WHAT IS MARRIAGE MADE OF?

This might sound strange to you, but I'll say it: *your marriage was made for this.*

It's popular to think that your marriage is protected by the strength of your feelings. What keeps you and your spouse married is that you stay "in love." Your feelings fortify your marriage. But, biblically, the reverse is true: your marriage is designed to fortify your faltering feelings.[1]

Your marriage is not built primarily on your feelings. That's not what holds it together. Your marriage is built on something that God has done. This is what Jesus says: "What therefore *God has joined together*, let not man separate" (Matt. 19:6). Marriage is made of much more durable stuff than the way that you feel when your spouse walks into the room. It's God's omnipotent power that joins you together and declares that you are one flesh—forever (see Gen. 2:24–25).

This is why we use the word *covenant* when we describe marriage. We are communicating that it is a permanent earthly relationship that is designed to endure through fickle feelings, arguments, suffering, parenting, money problems, and disease. We use the word *covenant* because we recognize that marriage is

---

1. My thoughts on this topic have been deeply shaped by John Piper's *This Momentary Marriage: A Parable of Permanence* (2009; repr., Wheaton, IL: Crossway, 2012).

God's doing—and we want to align ourselves with his design for this area of our lives.

You need to recognize this if you are going to experience hope that things can get better. Maybe you have been tempted to think that your waning feelings for your spouse mean that it isn't God's plan for you to stay together. That's a lie. God has already told you in his Word that he has joined you together and that he views you as being one flesh. We shouldn't be suspicious of God's Word; we should be suspicious of our feelings.

This is good news. It means that the all-powerful God himself is committed to your marriage. The unchanging God wants to help you with the changing feelings you are experiencing in these first years of your marriage. But how?

REMEMBER, REPENT, RENEW

God wants you to *remember* his purpose for marriage. Yes, he wants you and your spouse to remember that he brought you together, but he also wants you to remember his purpose for your marriage. God wants your marriage to display the gospel itself (see Eph. 5:22–33). You demonstrate this purpose in your day-to-day lives as you love, serve, and give yourself to each other.

At some point during your first years of marriage, you'll get forgetful. You will forget the great purpose of marriage and need to be reminded of it. You might also forget the promises you and your spouse made to each other before God and others. When this happens, go on a date night and spend some time *remembering*. Read Ephesians 5:22–33, read your vows together, and pray. Obviously, this isn't all you need to do—you also should reach out to trusted friends and to pastors in your church to ask for help while also trusting that God will help you as you commit to a biblical process of change. But the first step in making that commitment is to remember what God has done and the purpose that he has for your marriage. You'll be surprised at the sparks this will create between you and your spouse.

Reading that passage from Ephesians will remind you that anytime we look at God's Word, it exposes us. This should lead us to *repent*. One of the sins we commonly commit when we feel like we have "fallen out of love" is that we set our minds on the sins and shortcomings of our spouses. Maybe we have gotten into a habit of thinking of all the ways they annoy us, or maybe we meditate on all the things *they* could do to make the marriage better. Jesus wants us to honestly confront one another (see Matt. 18:15); but before we do, he wants us to assess ourselves and "take the log out of [our] own eye" (Matt. 7:5).

Are there ways in which you have neglected your spouse? What things have you done that have contributed to the ice that has formed around your marriage? Be eager to confess those things to your spouse, and then take practical steps of repentance.

As we turn away from the sin in our own hearts, we trust that Jesus will provide the grace that we need to love our spouses according to his Word. The goal here is *renewal*. Renewal doesn't necessarily revolve around a return to steamy feelings of love. It involves filling our minds with God's Word (see Rom. 12:2) so that we can act in loving ways toward our spouses (see 1 Peter 1:13). For you, this might mean making a list of all the reasons you are grateful for your spouse and intentionally thinking about them as you come home to your spouse each day. It might mean memorizing passages about marriage that help you to remember God's design for it.

The primary purpose of marriage is not for you to experience feelings of warmth and love every day. Just because you don't have the feelings that are associated with love does not mean that you have fallen out of love. It means that you are human. But your marriage is not merely human. God has brought you and your spouse together. The two of you are one flesh. Even if you feel that you have fallen out of love, you have not fallen out of your God-ordained covenant with each other. That's impossible. Only death will end the covenant of marriage. It's durable.

Your marriage was made for this. Remember, repent, renew—and watch omnipotent power come to your aid as you trust God's Word.

Until then,
Spencer

DISCUSSION QUESTIONS

1. In what ways have you developed "marriage amnesia"? What comes to your mind when you think about your spouse?
2. In what ways have you contributed to any "ice" that has formed around your marriage?
3. Share with your spouse three particular ways that you are grateful for him or her.

ON CHILDREN

Spencer and Taylor

Dear Romantic,

It was 6:00 a.m. We were both excited and a little nervous. Taylor had bought a pregnancy test the night before, and we had agreed that she would take it this morning. She took the test, and we put it facedown on the bathroom sink while it processed the results. We waited an eternal two minutes, closed our eyes, and flipped over the test. Positive! We gasped, hugged, looked at that test over and over again. We were in stunned disbelief.

We had been married for only three months.

Several months of terrible sickness later, after getting our apartment ready and holding a few baby showers, we greeted our firstborn daughter—just one week after our one-year wedding anniversary.

Seven months after that, we found out that we were pregnant with our second daughter. And, last year, we welcomed our third child (a son!) into our home. For those of you who are doing the math, that's three children in the first five years of marriage. We are one of the few couples in our group of friends who have had that many children in such a short time.

Here's the question: if you are able, should you do what we did?

BLESSING VS. BURDEN

You have probably noticed a spectrum of thought that people have regarding whether to have children during the first years of marriage.

Some people emphasize that children are a blessing, as we see in Psalm 127:3. Such people will point out that you are young and that you have energy and time, and that God says this is a blessing—so what are you waiting for?! Children bring so much joy, and you will grow closer to your spouse as you raise a child together. You feel the truth of what they are saying and wonder if you would be selfish if you waited a few years before having children.

Other people emphasize that children are a burden. They too would say that you are young and that you have energy and time—but they would argue that you should therefore enjoy your early years of marriage together. Children are wonderful, but they significantly change your life, your marriage, and your home. Don't you want to adjust to your newly married life? You don't need another burden on top of the major change that marriage brings. This point of view makes sense to you as well. It does seem like it would be a risk to introduce another life into your marriage when you're still trying to figure out the life you already have with your spouse. Perhaps you should continue using a contraceptive[1] and wait for a better time.

---

1. For biblical guidance on contraceptives, see Sean and Jenny Perron,

Perhaps you have felt the tension of these competing views. Which perspective is right? Which one is wise?

They both are.

THE BLESSED BURDEN

The unwavering teaching of Scripture is that children are a blessing. The Bible tells us that they are an inheritance from God himself and a reward that we receive, that they are like arrows for a warrior, and that they are an honor for us in the world (see Ps. 127:3–5). We see Abraham and Sarah longing for a son (see Gen. 16), Hannah praying fervently for a child (see 1 Sam. 1:9–11), and Jesus using children as a primary metaphor for how his followers must receive the kingdom (see Matt. 18:1–3). The way we think and talk about children should match what God has revealed to us about them—and should inform the priorities we have in our marriages.

However, that doesn't mean that children won't be a burden. Children can cause much trouble in the life of a parent. They can bring sorrow, grief, and shame (see Prov. 10:1; 17:25; 19:26). Parents also bear the responsibility of diligently teaching, training, and disciplining their children (see Deut. 6:7; Prov. 22:6; Eph. 6:4). Having children is a blessing, but it's not a blessing to pursue haphazardly.

These truths mean that children are a blessed burden. They can break your heart or bless your name for the rest of your days. Our approach to having children needs to take into account both of these truths from Scripture.

"On Birth Control," chap. 18 in Sean Perron and Spencer Harmon, *Letters to a Romantic: On Engagement* (Phillipsburg, NJ: P&R Publishing, 2017).

NOW OR LATER?

If children are a blessed burden, then the question most Christians are going to be asking is not *whether* they should have children but *when* it is wise for them to do so, if they are able to. Obviously, there is no direct command in Scripture about when couples should have children. However, God's Word speaks directly to one of the most common temptations that rises in our hearts when we approach such an important conversation.

God's Word forbids us to make decisions that are rooted in fear and anxiety. One of the most common refrains regarding having children that is repeated by couples who are in their early years of marriage is "We're just not ready yet!" This statement often isn't motivated by concrete and obvious reasons why it wouldn't be wise for them to have children but rather by a vague "what if?" mentality. "What if we don't have enough money? What if we miscarry? What if I'm a terrible parent? What if I lose my job? This is too risky!"

God calls us out of this "what if?" mentality and calls us instead to believe that he knows what we need and will provide it (see Matt. 6:31–32). God guards your heart and your mind in Christ as you give your burdens to him through prayer (see Phil. 4:6–7). He calls us all to trust his provision, and even to take faith-filled risks, as we navigate our futures. This all means that you can trust him to provide what you need in the area of parenting in particular, and it also means that you can rejoice in an unplanned pregnancy that you are tempted to be nervous about.

This does not mean, however, that there are no reasons why we might wait to have children. God wants us to be thoughtful about the decisions that we make (see Prov. 15:14). It can be wise for a person to forego something that they know will be joyful now so that they can prepare themselves to receive it later (see Prov. 6:6–11).

You and your spouse, while deeply desiring to have children, may decide that for the first few years you want to develop healthy family habits together before introducing a new life into your home. Your first season of marriage may even have been extremely difficult, and thus you also want to get help from a trusted pastor or friend before starting your family. Maybe you or your spouse has a medical issue that you need to get more clarity on before you try to have children. You may be finishing school and want to complete a degree so that you will be better able to provide for a child. Couples are free to wisely navigate these issues while at the same time desiring and prizing children in their home.

The common thread throughout all the wise reasons why you might delay having children is selflessness. You are seeking to serve your spouse by taking health concerns into account before you get pregnant. You are seeking to serve your child by dealing with some significant and specific problems in your marriage. God cares about your heart. He cares about *why* you do or don't want children.[2]

Children are a blessing from the Lord. As we have seen, that is because they are arrows in our hand—a gift that we receive from God himself. But they are also a blessing because they provide a small window into the kingdom (see Mark 10:15). They often model the humility, joy, and sincerity that God wants all his people to be marked by.

The joy of children is that, while you are training them, they

---

2. This also applies to the issue of adoption and foster care. God cares about *why* we want to adopt or foster. He wants our hearts to be motivated by service and selflessness—not by self-promotion or other selfish desires.

are also training you. As you consider the gift that children are, our prayer is that your heart would be marked by the childlike humility, joy, and sincerity that God desires in you.

Until then,
Spencer and Taylor

DISCUSSION QUESTIONS

1. Do you overemphasize the ways in which children are either a blessing or a burden? Explain.
2. If you are struggling with whether you should wait to have children, what are your reasons? Are they motivated by a desire to serve?
3. What are your fears about having children? Discuss them with your spouse.

COMMUNICATING ABOUT SEX

Sean and Jenny

Dear Romantic,

When you are married, there are numerous things that need to be discussed on a regular basis. How was work? How are the kids? What are our plans for the week? What do you want to eat? How was sex tonight?

Does that last question feel shocking to you? The fact is that in order to glorify God and properly love your spouse through sex, you must speak about it with him or her. It can't remain unaddressed.

How can you have meaningful conversations about sex with your spouse? You should be sure to address wants, worries, ways, and whys.

WANTS AND WORRIES

God has designed sex to be an intimate time of togetherness for you and your spouse. It is the closest relationship that two humans can possibly have. There is no other time when you are so connected and intertwined. It is a beautiful thing that should result in transparency, unity, and unhindered affection.

For this reason, sexual desires should not remain silent. If a spouse wants to enjoy something during sex, it should at least be discussed. A spouse should be free to voice what they like and dislike and to bring up any number of desires or preferences regarding sex. For example, a wife may desire that her husband slow down during sex and enjoy her less sexual parts. She might want him to stroke her hair or face. She might enjoy him being more verbal about why he finds her attractive. Or she may want him to stop caressing her in one area and start massaging her in another. A husband may want to try a different sexual position. Maybe he doesn't care about getting a massage, but he loves it when his wife wears lingerie.

Start the conversation by asking questions. What do you like when we have sex? What could you live without? What is your favorite thing? What is your least favorite?

It isn't enough to talk only about wants; you have to talk about worries as well. What hopes and fears do you each have regarding sex? Do you have any concerns about each other's likes and dislikes?

It could be that a wife worries about wearing a specific garment because she is self-conscious. She fears that her appearance won't be appreciated or doesn't think that she is beautiful. Perhaps a wife is worried that a particular desire is trashy. Maybe her husband wants to enjoy oral sex, but it feels dirty to her.

A husband may wish that his wife would initiate sex more often but may not want to appear passive or too eager for sex. Or it is possible for a husband to worry about whether his wife enjoys sex at all but to be too nervous to bring up the issue. The wife could also be the one who wants more but doesn't want to appear to be too sensual.

Worries must be discussed or they will never be worked through. Talk about both your and your spouse's likes and dislikes.

There are many different ways that you can enjoy the marriage bed. Explore them together and enjoy each other in the ways that your spouse desires. Loving each other involves both of you assuming the best about each other and not assuming the worst about each other's desires (see 1 Cor. 13:7)—don't jump to the conclusion that a preference to try something new in the bedroom comes from a place of dissatisfaction or sinful inspiration. Live with each other in an understanding way and outdo each other in kindness (see Rom. 12:10; 1 Peter 3:7).

WAYS AND WHYS

All these wants and worries lead to ways and whys. What *ways* should a couple have sex and *why*? Here are some biblical guidelines.

The ways must be determined by an exclusive covenant.[1] God has established the parameters of sex. It should take place only between one man and one woman until death alone separates them. This is the way for the marriage bed to remain undefiled (see Heb. 13:4). So using anyone else's body for any sexual activity is forbidden and will bring God's judgment. It is sinful to bring another person into the marriage bed—whether physically, virtually, or mentally. Adultery is the most obvious act that is off-limits (see Ex. 20:14), and pornography is not permitted either. Even if both spouses are comfortable with using

1. See Sean Perron and Spencer Harmon, *Letters to a Romantic: On Engagement* (Phillipsburg, NJ: P&R Publishing, 2017), 108.

pornography as part of their sexual activity, God is not okay with it under any circumstance. Using lustful thoughts to bring about an orgasm, whether they come from pornography, your imagination, or personal memories, is unbiblical (see Matt. 5:28; contrast with Phil. 4:8). God wants you to be present with your spouse and to love the one you are with.

If you want to bring a third party into the marriage bed, why? Are you not content with your current relationship? Are you looking for a forbidden thrill?

Our answers to these questions expose our idolatry for things that are contrary to God's Word and his ways. God loves to bless faithfulness and is ready to forgive. Repent of any lustful desires you have and submit yourself to the lordship of Christ. The Holy Spirit can give you desires that are exclusively for your spouse.

The ways must be acceptable to both husband and wife. Both a husband and a wife must agree on the ways they are having sex. If either person is uncomfortable with how one of them is experiencing an orgasm, then there is a problem. The Bible says that whatever is done must be done in faith (see Rom. 14:23) and cannot violate anyone's conscience.

There are sexual things that the Bible does not forbid but that might not be everyone's preference.[2] If a husband wants his

2. Our position is that if the Bible does not forbid something related to sex, then it is permitted as long as it doesn't violate other biblical principles or parameters. For example, it is our view that oral sex is not forbidden by God and can be done to the praise of his glory. We believe it is in keeping with Song of Solomon 2:3, 16 and 4:16–5:1. This is not the case for anal sex, because although the Bible doesn't explicitly forbid it, it is in violation of the biblical principle that we should not harm or damage one another. It is a reality that our bodies were not designed for anal sex, and it risks inflicting injury. See also Perron and Harmon, *Letters to a Romantic: On Engagement,* 116–19, where we address the issue of oral sex.

wife to stimulate him with her mouth but she doesn't feel comfortable doing so, this verse considers the issue to be settled. That desire should be dropped like a hot potato. Oral sex isn't required by God. If either a husband or wife are uncomfortable with something related to sex, then it should be cast into the abyss of forgetfulness. The point of sex isn't to force a desire upon your spouse; it is to serve your spouse so that you bring them joy. The whole point of sexual union is to display the gospel.[3] Love does not insist on its own way (see 1 Cor. 13:5).[4]

The *why* question is very important to ask in relation to these issues. Truly examine your own heart before trying to help your spouse (see Matt. 7:5). When you read the following questions, evaluate yourself—not your spouse.

If you are desirous of something that your spouse doesn't want, why do you want it so badly? If you are having a hard time giving up your preferences, why is that? Are those preferences an idol? If so, repent. Believe that Jesus forgives you and gives you the power to replace your idol with God's design and desires.

If you are uncomfortable with something related to sex, why does it make you uncomfortable? Do you need to have

3. Paul conveys in Ephesians 5 that the mystery of the gospel is displayed within both the marriage covenant and the marriage bed. And in 1 Corinthians 6:16–17, in addition to directly quoting Genesis 2:24, he uses the language "joined to the Lord," which is the same as the phrase "hold fast" in that verse from Genesis. (The ESV's footnote at verse 16 is helpful for seeing this connection with Genesis, as well as with another verse from Deuteronomy.) The sexual joining—or "holding fast"—that makes a husband and wife one flesh also symbolizes the joining of a believer and the Lord, who become one spirit. See Perron and Harmon, *Letters to a Romantic: On Engagement*, 109; for additional specific details on how sex mirrors the gospel, see all of chapter 19, "On Sex."

4. If you believe that your spouse is being manipulative and is unwilling to repent of it, you will need to get outside help. Although it may be difficult, you will need to reach out to a godly couple, a pastor, or a counselor in your church.

your conscience informed by the Bible? Do you need further thought regarding this area—or perhaps renewal, if you have been affected by a past experience? Or is this an area you are truly convinced is off-limits, even in marriage (see Rom. 14:5)?

The ways must be safe and sacred. Sex was never intended by God to be a cheap throwaway act. He designed sex to be sweet and secure. He wants it to be a precious gift for married couples to enjoy. It is a delight that couples are to treasure, for the glory of Christ, in the sacred and secure bonds of the marriage covenant (see 1 Tim. 4:3–4).

This means any sexual activity that is painful, inherently risky, or forced is unacceptable. Sex should be an act of love, not one that brings about harm—we should treat our spouses as we would want to be treated (see Luke 6:31). Couples should thus not attempt any sexual act that could cause damage. This excludes anal sex as an option.

If at any time sex is painful for either person, you should stop the position and try a new one. Do everything you can to help your spouse to enjoy sex pain-free.

The ways must not be self-stimulated. The Bible does not require spouses to climax simultaneously, although that is certainly a fine thing. But whenever a spouse does climax, it should be because the other spouse brought them to sexual satisfaction. This can occur through various ways and at various times during sex, but an orgasm should not be self-obtained.

To be as clear as possible, a husband's climax should be brought about by his wife, not by his hand. And the same applies for a wife. If a husband is on a business trip, it is not godly for him to masturbate even if he is looking at naked photos of his wife or if she is on a video call with him. If a wife is at home while her husband is away, it is wrong for her to stimulate herself even if she is thinking about him. Toys and masturbation have no place in a marriage, because biblical sex was never designed to be self-performed in any capacity. This is because sex should be selfless rather than selfish (see Phil. 2:4)—its purpose is to delight in your spouse alone, not in anything else that might bring about pleasure. We are called by God to control our bodies in holiness and honor instead of in passionate lust like unbelievers (see 1 Thess. 4:1–8). To bring yourself to climax removes your spouse's role in the sex act and undercuts the picture that marriage is supposed to portray of Christ and the church (see Eph. 5:31–32). Sex is designed to be a sweet, selfless experience that is shared by both a husband and a wife.

The main way should be intercourse. Intercourse (which can occur in a variety of ways and positions) should be the primary way by which couples bring about sexual fulfillment. Unless there is a physical or medical reason for them to do so, it isn't good for the more unusual methods of sexual satisfaction to replace intercourse.[5] We don't want to adopt the false idea that the more atypical sex is, the more thrilling it is—an idea that comes from our culture's unhealthy fixation on the exotic. This misses the point of sex entirely.

But at the same time, sex isn't meant to be boring. It is meant to be a blast. We hope that you find the marriage bed to be one of the best places in the world. It should be more thrilling than an amusement park. You should find so much sexual pleasure

---

5. If you are continually replacing intercourse with oral sex or manual stimulation, why? Are you bored? What is appealing about the other ways of sex that leads you to neglect intercourse in favor of them? Examine your heart to see whether you are fixating on an idol and need to have your mind renewed (see Rom. 12:1–2).

in your spouse that you can be described as being "intoxicated" with love (Prov. 5:19; see also Song 5:1).

Be creative, innovative, and intoxicated—but don't be fixated on the particulars of sex to a fault. Being obsessed with a particular element of sex or with the next level of it only demonstrates an unbiblical infatuation with your preference for experiencing pleasure—which is idolatry. Seek instead to glorify God in all things and above all things.

It is more than okay to have ordinary sex. Sometimes sex will be amazing, and sometimes it won't. Sometimes it will be "as dramatic as a thunderstorm, sometimes as comfortable and unemphatic as putting on your soft slippers."[6] And that is good.

God loves to bless faithfulness. He loves to give his children delight in his good gifts and to reward them for their contentment. If you are always looking for the next thrill, then you don't understand true pleasure. Godliness with contentment is great gain—and this applies to sex just as much as the Bible says it does to money (see Phil. 4:12–13; 1 Tim. 6:6).

The grass isn't greener on the other side of the fence, and sex won't be more fulfilling in another person's bed. The grass is greenest where God's blessing resides. His presence, favor, and happiness are with those who follow his Word. God wants you to have lots of sex with your spouse, and the kind of sex he wants you to have is the kind that is most pleasurable and eternally rewarding.

Keep the marriage bed pure and precious—and please keep talking.

Until then,
Sean and Jenny

6. C. S. Lewis, *A Grief Observed* (New York: HarperCollins, 1994), 7.

DISCUSSION QUESTIONS

1. What are your sexual wants? Why do you want them?
2. What are your spouse's sexual wants? Why does he or she want them?
3. What are your sexual worries? What are your spouse's sexual worries?
4. When was the last time you talked about sex with your spouse?

FREQUENCY OF SEX

Sean and Jenny

Dear Romantic,

Satan wants you to have less sex. God wants you to have more.

I'm not exaggerating. Real spiritual warfare is taking place in your bedroom. Notice what Paul writes: "Do not deprive one another [sexually], except perhaps by agreement for a limited time, that you may devote yourselves to prayer; but then come together again, so that *Satan* may not tempt you because of your lack of self-control" (1 Cor. 7:5).

The devil tempts couples to have sex *before* marriage, but then he wants them to refrain from sex *after* marriage.[1] Satan himself does this so that we will be tempted to forsake our vows.

God, however, wants couples to abstain from sex before marriage—which leads to death—and then to enjoy frequent sex within marriage, which brings life. He commands this so that we will be satisfied and will walk in the reward of righteousness.

---

1. We learned this, and many of the practical applications of 1 Corinthians 7 that are found in this chapter, from Heath and Lauren Lambert during our premarital counseling.

SEX ISN'T ULTIMATELY ABOUT YOUR BODY

God created sex with many purposes—and ultimately to be for our good and his glory.[2] He cares about the bedroom, because he cares about us. He cares about how often we make love, because he loves to see us delight in his good gifts.

We were bought with an extreme price so that we would glorify God with our bodies—which includes our sex (see 1 Cor. 6:20).[3] God doesn't want our hearts to be deceived to pursue immorality; he wants them to be devoted to our Savior first and our spouses second.

God is concerned about what you are doing with your body sexually because he is concerned about what you are doing with your soul spiritually.

Sex within marriage is not a power play.

The husband should give to his wife her conjugal rights, and likewise the wife to her husband. For the wife does not have authority over her own body, but the husband does. Likewise the husband does not have authority over his own body, but the wife does. (1 Cor. 7:3–4)

Sex is designed to be an act of sweet service to your spouse. God wants you to delight in your spouse so much that you overwhelm them with sexual love.

A truly vibrant sexual relationship can happen only between two people who are deeply in love with each other and with the

2. See Sean Perron, "On Sex," chap. 19 in Sean Perron and Spencer Harmon, *Letters to a Romantic: On Engagement* (Phillipsburg, NJ: P&R Publishing, 2017).

3. See Denny Burk, *What Is the Meaning of Sex?* (Wheaton, IL: Crossway, 2013), 119.

Lord. A healthy sexual relationship is possible only when two people have hearts that love to worship God above all else.

PRACTICAL DETAILS

So how often should you have sex? I think the question is phrased incorrectly. Instead of asking how often you and your spouse should have sex, you should ask how often you can *serve* your spouse with sex.

At the beginning of marriage, couples typically have a lot of sex. Eventually, that rate of sexual activity unavoidably drops. Life happens, work picks up, routines go back to normal. How can couples best adjust to the reduced frequency of sex that takes place during normal life after they have experienced the out-of-this-world frequency of sex during their first weeks of marriage?

Sex should be prioritized and planned. When life gets busy, couples stay clothed. The way to combat this is to make sex a priority. It can't be an afterthought.

By way of analogy, everyone winds up eating during the day. Somehow, someway, people eat each day no matter how busy life gets. Why? It is a priority for us. You and your spouse must believe that sex is likewise a priority. It should be such a priority for you that a week without sex is a big deal. Any extended time in which you don't have sex should be something that you both decide on as an intentional strategy.[4]

Have you and your spouse talked about this? Sit down

---

4. Strategically refraining from sex is permitted only for the purpose of prayer, and only as long as it is mutually beneficial and agreed upon (see 1 Cor. 7:5). Other necessary constraints might also keep a couple from sex for a time, such as postpartum recovery, work trips, deployment, a brief time of having to be separate in order to care for sick family members, and so on. But these times without it should always be temporary and as short as possible.

together and discuss how often you want to have sex during a typical week. It might be twice a week; it might be four times a week—but however often sex happens, it should be treated as a mutually acknowledged priority that flows from *love*.

Some people think that planning sex saps all the romance out of it—that it must be spontaneous in order to be sensual. False. The best things in life are usually planned. Think about the greatest vacation you have ever taken. Did you plan for that vacation? Absolutely. You took time off work. You booked the hotel. You planned the tours. Even if your dream vacation was to sit by the pool and read a book, you still had to plan for that. If we plan our vacations so that we can enjoy them, we should not be afraid that plans and dates will ruin the romance in our marriages.[5]

Maybe you could designate Tuesday and Thursday nights as "naked nights." Or maybe, instead of planning a specific date or time, you could plan to have sex at least once every three days. Scheduling spontaneous sex can be sexy. You can be creative with your calendar as long as that calendar gives sex the attention it deserves.[6]

---

5. See Heath Lambert and Brad Bigney, "Glorifying God In Your Sexual Relationship," April 5, 2017, in *Truth in Love*, produced by Association of Certified Biblical Counselors, podcast, mp3 audio, 13:14, https://biblical counseling.com/til-087-glorifying-god-sexual-relationship-feat-brad -bigney/.

6. There is freedom for spouses to enjoy each other in a variety of ways, as long as none of those ways violate either spouse's conscience or harm them physically. The issue of climaxing without intercourse is an important part of the conversation about how frequently sex should happen—especially when it comes to situations like postpartum recovery. Husbands and wives should discuss their expectations regarding sex during the postpartum period in advance. Even though they should avoid intercourse for weeks after labor, there are other ways that spouses can satisfy each other sexually until it is medically permissible for them to resume intercourse.

SEX FOR GOD'S GLORY

God isn't a prude. He created sex to be thrilling, and he gave it to us as a gift. Gifts are fun. Gifts bring joy. We like gifts and want more of them. Each spouse should ask themselves, "Am I seeking for God to use me to bring sexual gifts to my spouse?" Or better yet, spouses should ask each other, "Is God using me to bring you sexual gifts?"

Proverbs 5:15–20 teaches us that we should be satisfied sexually with our spouses, which is the clear implication of 1 Corinthians 7 as well.[7] The "marriage bed" is to remain undefiled (Heb. 13:4). Couples who are satisfied with each other don't seek sex outside of wedlock—regular sex continually purifies the marriage bed and helps to fight against sexual impurity.

But the *act* of frequent sex in marriage doesn't curb temptation on its own. You must find pleasure in Jesus before you will be able to find it in bed. Glorifying God is to be the source of your happiness (see 1 Cor. 10:31). You can have consistent climaxes and still have a heart that is discontent. Sex is more than just a bodily act.

Your entire person is designed to be engaged in sex. When your heart is thrilled with, and thankful for, what happens in bed; when your mind is self-controlled when you are in the sheets; and when your will is selflessly serving your spouse first; your temptation will be weakened.

The couples who guard their marriage bed are those who are

---

7. While 1 Corinthians 7 teaches that spouses should not sin against each other by withholding sex, it does not teach that withholding sex from a spouse *causes* that spouse to look for it elsewhere and commit adultery. There is never a biblical reason, or one based on biological need, for seeking sex outside of marriage.

enthralled with God first and with each other second. As they seek to worship God with all their hearts, minds, and souls, their bodies will come together often. Frequent sex in marriage is a beautiful thing, and it pleases God. He loves to see you love your spouse as yourself (see Luke 10:27).

Until then,
Sean and Jenny

DISCUSSION QUESTIONS

1. How often do you and your spouse have sex?
2. Do you want to have more sex? Does your spouse want to have more sex?
3. Is sex a priority in your marriage? Why or why not? If a busy schedule prevents this from happening, how can you plan to overcome that schedule in order to make it a priority?

SEXUAL DIFFICULTY
FOR HUSBANDS

Sean

Dear Romantic,

It is hard to find people in the church today who will admit that sex isn't always sexy.

The truth is that sex can be difficult, complicated, and confusing.

Ever since sin entered the world, sex has been a struggle. Mankind fell, and so did the marriage bed. The good news is that God came to redeem every part of humanity (see Col. 1:20), and that includes what happens between the sheets.

No problem is too personal for Jesus. No difficulty is too deep for God. His Word gives guidance regarding sexual problems. He is eager for married couples to delight in each other—naked and unashamed (see Gen. 2:25).

The next two letters will address two sexual problems that are physical in nature. One is focused on the husband, and the other is focused on the wife. Both husband and wife should read each of these letters in order to understand the problems and solutions that they discuss.

RESOURCES FOR DIFFICULTIES

A sexual problem that husbands can face in the first years of marriage is the issue of erectile dysfunction. Some husbands have no problem with sexual arousal. They are turned on before the lights are turned off. But when wives come into the bedroom with a playful glance and start to undress, some husbands feel fear being aroused instead of excitement.

This difficulty can plague husbands. "Why can't I get an erection?" "What is wrong with me?" "Am I not attracted to my wife?" Fear, embarrassment, and confusion can consume their thoughts.

There are at least three kinds of factors that can contribute to a husband's difficulty with gaining or maintaining an erection: circumstantial, internal, and medical.

Circumstantial. Stress related to external circumstances is a contributor to physical sexual difficulty. Are there any stressors that could be contributing to your heart feeling occupied? Is work overwhelming you? Are family dynamics weighing you down?

We are not merely material bodies; we are embodied souls. Our circumstances can impact our hearts and take a physical toll on us. We are not controlled by those circumstances, but they can certainly contribute to the stress that we feel.

The good news is that our circumstances can never *cause* us to be anxious or to sin (see 1 Cor. 10:13). Anxiety and sin ultimately come from our hearts (see Mark 7:21–22; Luke 6:45). This is good news, because our hearts can know the peace of the Holy Spirit—God's eternal presence, which he gives us and which steadies us in the midst of our stress and overcomes our anxiety.

Internal. Trouble in the soul can impact a husband's performance in bed. Tensions, sins, and relational weaknesses can paralyze him sexually.

Fear is the most common factor in erectile dysfunction.[1] Fear pushes out all excitement. It throws a bucket of ice water on the fire of holy sensuality. A husband may fear that he isn't attracted to his wife. He may be anxious because she wants more sex than he can give. If he couldn't get an erection once before, he may now worry that it will happen again.

Closely related to fear is sadness or despair. A husband who is despairing about an aspect of his life might carry that sadness over into his sex life. Humans have a hard time compartmentalizing inner turmoil, and one despairing domino can hit another.

Conflict within marriage can also contribute to sexual dysfunction. Relational angst isn't a recipe for arousal. Frustration with your wife, anxiety about an upcoming decision that the two of you disagree about, or a mind that is preoccupied with replaying conversations with her will hinder sex.

Past or present sexual sin can be a factor as well. Husbands who have a history of pornography usage might have trouble getting quickly aroused by a real-life woman. Those who have struggled with same-sex attraction might have fear about and

---

1. See Ed Wheat and Gaye Wheat, *Intended for Pleasure: Sex Technique and Sexual Fulfillment in Christian Marriage*, 4th ed. (Grand Rapids: Revell, 2010), 128, 134. The book lacks a robust biblical counseling framework and sometimes incorporates unhelpful therapeutic elements, but I recommend it for the practical sexual advice it offers to Christian couples who are experiencing problems related to performance.

difficulty with performing well for their wives. Husbands who have been sexually abused could also have challenges with this issue—a traumatic sexual experience or a painful memory can have an ongoing impact on a person's view of sex.[2]

If you are experiencing erectile dysfunction, there could be numerous internal factors contributing to it, and they will be specific to you. If you are able to identify an internal struggle you are having, it can be your first step toward making progress with this issue. It could very well be a mixture of factors like fear, worry, sexual sin, despair, or stress. Identifying these internal issues and working through them with biblical truth and wisdom will bring you relief.

Some husbands can't pinpoint an exact cause for their sexual difficulties. All too often our internal turmoil is intertwined and hard to unravel. I would caution against introspection that causes you to jump to conclusions about the source of your struggle.[3] Both husbands and wives can feel the temptation to fear the worst—to assume that difficulties are being caused by something more worrisome, or even sinful, than they actually are—and this can heighten the intensity of their situation.

If the cause of your difficulty is unclear, it won't be helpful for you to worry and obsess over tracking it down. Why? The more you fear losing an erection, the more you will "fail." The internal cycle of fear can be hard to break. It can feel like a strong

2. See the resources under the "Abuse" section of the recommended resources list at the back of this book for help and counsel regarding this area.

3. Although it will be uncomfortable and difficult, you should talk about this issue with a godly, mature man whom you trust. Trying to avoid the problem will only make it worse. Getting a third party to help you to understand the issues you are dealing with will be clarifying and helpful. Don't let embarrassment keep you miserable. Reach out to a trusted friend who can give his honest evaluation of your struggles.

rip current. The more you tell yourself *not* to fear, the more you may fear. The more you struggle against the waves, the more panic can flood your soul. The solution for sexual difficulties isn't going to be found purely through introspection. It is going to be found in the gospel of Jesus Christ, which, we will see, frees us from our fear.

Medical. A medical factor can cause or contribute to erectile dysfunction. A variety of issues such as heart disease, high cholesterol, or high blood pressure may hinder your ability to perform. If you have ruled out circumstantial and internal causes, then getting a medical checkup would be wise and warranted. There is no shame in scheduling an appointment with your doctor.

SUGGESTIONS FOR REAL CHANGE

What are some practical steps that married couples can take in order to make progress in this area?

Bear with each other in bed. Bearing with each other means that spouses should extend charity, humility, love, kindness, grace, sympathy, gentleness, and mercy to each other (see Eph. 4:2). When couples take the biblical posture of forbearance, they will begin to make progress through sexual difficulties. Erectile dysfunction can be embarrassing for a husband, and there is a deep peace that comes when he can know that his wife is being understanding. It is crucial for a wife to be patient and willing to work through this issue if a husband is going to make progress.

Release steam before trying to release semen. Patience and peace are fruits of the Spirit and of great value in your sexual relationship (see 1 Cor. 13:4; Gal. 5:22). Since fear and stress are common causes of erectile dysfunction, removing some of the pressure they cause can help to cultivate peace. The anticipation before and build-up to the moment of sex can contribute to a husband's feeling an expectation to come through and not to mess up.

You may find it refreshing to be reminded that you can have precious encounters in bed without an expectation of climaxing. This change of perspective releases steam from the pressure cooker that a husband can feel. Couples can remove this tension by loving each other and allowing for authentic pleasure to surface. It is reassuring for a husband to know that his wife accepts him regardless of his performance.

Husband, if your wife is bearing with you in bed and is being patient and understanding, then the pressure is off. You don't have to perform. You have been freed up to enjoy her in a slow and significant way. As your wife cultivates the fruit of patience, you can cultivate the fruit of peace.

This patience and peace come from fixing our eyes on the Lord and trusting him to empower us. Believers' position in Christ is secure because of Jesus's perfect life, death, and resurrection. We don't have to perform in order to earn our standing before God (Eph. 2:8–10).

Lose yourself in order to find yourself. This principle is derived from Luke 17:33. Focusing on yourself is the way to bring about sexual failure. Focusing on your spouse is the way to find sexual fulfillment. No one's identity should be wrapped up in his ability to obtain and maintain an erection.

Your focus should be on pleasing your spouse and delighting in them. Husband, discover what things your wife would enjoy in bed that don't involve an erection. When your attention is on arousing your wife, you just might become stimulated, yourself, in the process. Seek to climax her in whatever way she desires. If being slowly and tenderly stimulated to climax isn't the type of sexual experience she would like, then think together about ways to show her thoughtful love in this area.

Cultivate thankfulness. Your wife's worth is not tied to sex. (And neither is yours!) Cultivate an exclusive, pure sexual desire for your wife, but don't think about her *only* in a sexual way. Cultivate thankfulness for her in a holistic way.

Thank God for your wife's entire body. Prize her nonsexual parts when you are in bed. Enjoy the parts of her that are often overlooked—as well as her inner parts that are invisible (see 1 Peter 3:4). Spend time snuggling with her. Take time to caress her. Spend your day cultivating a heart of gratitude (see Col. 3:15), not dreading what will—or *won't!*—happen in bed that night.

Take the gospel to bed with you. Think about how God treats us. He is patient with us. He is loving, and he casts out our fear (see 1 John 4:18). He loves to serve. He doesn't draw undue focus to our areas of struggle. He doesn't treat us harshly when we are suffering from sickness or physical weakness. He doesn't condemn us even when we are at fault (see Rom. 8:1).

Jesus repeatedly told his disciples to "Fear not!" If you are fearful of the marriage bed, repent of this fear and ask Jesus for forgiveness and grace. Trust that his blood is sufficient to wash you from all your sinful worries. Ask him to give you the power to overcome all your anxiety as well as bold faith regarding the marriage bed. Even if you are concerned because you can't determine the exact cause of your issues and feel all too aware of your own weakness, continue to believe the good news of Jesus. He is your Savior, Shepherd, and Friend.

Whatever emotions and troubles you are experiencing related to this issue, Jesus is a kind Shepherd. He knows exactly what troubles us. He will make us lie down in green pastures and will lead us beside peaceful waters. He restores our souls and guarantees that goodness and mercy will follow us all the days of our lives.

You can trust him—not just regarding this particular problem with sex but also regarding every problem you will face as a couple.

Until then,
Sean

DISCUSSION QUESTIONS

1. What are the factors (whether circumstantial, internal, or medical) that you think could be contributing to your sexual difficulty?
2. If fear is a contributing factor, what passages of Scripture can help to renew your mind and put your fear to death?
3. What are some qualities and characteristics of your wife that you can enjoy and think about during the day?

SEXUAL DIFFICULTY FOR WIVES

Sean and Jenny

Dear Romantic,

All too often sexual struggles remain silent and in the shadows. It is important for us to directly address a struggle that is common for wives: difficulty climaxing during sex. This issue can lead to weeks, months, and even years of trouble and bitterness for couples.

Some wives have a short sexual on-ramp, and climaxing is a quick and frequent occurrence for them. Other wives have never experienced a sexual climax or have experienced it only as a rare phenomenon. How should a Christian couple work through this difficulty?

IS THERE A PROBLEM?

Some couples might wonder whether there is an issue if a wife doesn't experience an orgasm during sex. Is this a real problem?

The goal of biblical sex is to bring glory to God (see 1 Cor. 10:31). And bringing glory to God brings joy to us. When we honor God, we are filled with happiness from the Holy Spirit.[1] This means that God intends for every sexual encounter to be an enjoyable experience. But sex isn't simple—and we shouldn't have a simplistic view of it.

A wife can enjoy sex for the glory of God without experiencing a physical orgasm. Her heart can be full of thankfulness for the experience of being close to and held by her husband. She may enjoy passionate kissing and a thousand other pleasures in bed. A wife can also take true delight in pleasing her husband sexually even if she herself doesn't reach a physical climax.

The Bible does not require a husband and a wife to have an orgasm during every sexual experience. The true climax of scriptural sex isn't a physical one. The height of every enjoyment is actually worshipping God. The best earthly pleasures that we experience are made richer and deeper when we enjoy them for God's glory. He is our ultimate satisfaction in life, and when we enjoy the gift of sex to the praise of his glory, we are enjoying sex as it was designed to be experienced.[2] The ultimate goal of sex isn't to have an orgasm but to bring glory to God.

Yet, even if climaxing isn't the ultimate goal of every sexual experience, we should always seek to provide our spouses with the full *opportunity* to experience an orgasm (see Prov. 5:18; Eccl. 9:9; Song 4:12–16).[3] Your desire should be to bring physi-

---

1. For more information about how honoring God in the Christian life brings us happiness, see John Piper, *The Dangerous Duty of Delight: Daring to Make God Your Greatest Desire* (Colorado Springs: Multnomah Books, 2011) and Joe Rigney, *The Things of Earth: Treasuring God by Enjoying His Gifts* (Wheaton, IL: Crossway, 2015).

2. This chapter assumes the theology of sex as described in Sean Perron, "On Sex," chap. 19 in Sean Perron and Spencer Harmon, *Letters to a Romantic: On Engagement* (Phillipsburg, NJ: P&R Publishing, 2017).

3. The underlying assumption of Song of Solomon is that faith-filled covenantal sex is pleasurable. Giving your spouse the opportunity to climax obeys

cal fulfillment to your spouse. If for some reason a wife does not want to climax, that is fine; but she should be given the opportunity to do so by her husband.

If a wife is regularly unable to experience an orgasm, that is an issue for the couple to work through together. It should not be swept under the bed. A husband and wife should work together so that both of them are fully sexually satisfied.

REASONS FOR DIFFICULTIES

A wife may have difficulty in this area for various reasons. Relational, medical, and personal factors are three common types to consider.

Relational. Sex is a relational act. God did not create it to be mechanical or robotic. Humans have emotions, thoughts, feelings, and souls, and thus relational dynamics are an important part of experiencing an orgasm.

For example, a wife might have trouble climaxing because of relational tensions in the marriage. This turmoil can muddy the waters of sex. Instead of being a clear, beautiful lake of romance, sex can be disturbed by pollution that marital conflict introduces to the environment.

Emotional stress and inner turmoil often impact the romance that takes place in bed. It is said that sex doesn't start in the bedroom—the desires and thoughts that lead to the sexual act are an important part of the hours that lead up to it. A conflict in the morning can impact what happens in the evening. Conflict

---

the biblical command to love your neighbor as yourself (see Mark 12:31). It is best to assume that your spouse wants to climax instead of assuming otherwise, and thus it would be unloving not to give him or her the opportunity to do so.

in the home leads to complications in bed. Frustrations, anger, bitterness, sadness, confusion, and miscommunication can all impact a wife's sexual life.

Personal. Some wives never reach an orgasm because they have an unbiblical view of sex or have had terrible experiences in the past. During sex, they feel dirty, used, or unattractive. The epic poetry of romantic love that they see in Song of Solomon seems distant, unfamiliar, or out of touch with their personal experience. Past experiences or personal perspectives on sex can contribute to these views and feelings.

Another reason why a wife may not be sexually fulfilled is that she is too focused on her performance. Consider the following thoughts that can hinder an orgasm:

- "How am I doing? I really want this to be going well."
- "What is he thinking about me?"
- "I hope he doesn't notice _____. I wish my body were different."
- "I feel selfish for wanting him to do _____ for me. He probably doesn't want this."

All of these thoughts are focused on the self at some level. They cause a wife to place a burden on herself to perform well in bed or make her concerned that her husband will not enjoy her.

Or a wife's trouble with climaxing may have nothing to do with her theology, history, or concerns about her performance, but may just stem from the daily realities of her life. She may experience sexual difficulty because her mind is preoccupied. It could be focused on taking care of the house, the children, the bills, the in-laws, the church, the neighbors, or the social media accounts. It could be filled with thoughts about either harmless things or horrible things. Whatever details are occupying her mind, they present a distraction. A wife whose mind is elsewhere while her body goes through the motions of sex won't experience the pleasure of an orgasm.

Medical. Sex should not be painful. When a wife has sex for the first time, penetration can bring discomfort and mild pain. This pain should pass as the vagina stretches with more sex. A husband should always be gentle when he enters his wife. Slow is the way to go.

This initial discomfort is very different from a regular experience of pain during sex. If you are experiencing prolonged pain, then something is wrong. It is not normal for sex to be painful.

If you are experiencing pain during intercourse, please see a physician. We have known women who suffered unnecessarily for months. They were nowhere close to being able to experience an orgasm because of pain. This should not be. There are numerous medical factors that can cause intercourse to hurt. These medical issues can be addressed by a doctor and should not be overlooked.

Any of these areas, or a mixture of them, could lead to a difficult marriage bed. Thankfully, there are practical and biblical steps a couple can take so that a wife can know the pleasure of sexual fulfillment.

SUGGESTIONS FOR REAL CHANGE

Acknowledge and address the issue. Silence doesn't help sensuality. Don't remain silent. It is essential that married couples talk about these things. If there are relational problems in your marriage, reach out for help. If burdensome and heavy matters are occupying your mind, don't bear the weight of them alone (see Gal. 6:2).

A husband should ask a lot of questions with care, patience, and a willingness to help. He should ask his wife how he can put her at ease. The wife can then talk about her desires, what might be hindering her from enjoying sex, and what sexual things she loves the most. Never be afraid to reach out to a godly couple in your church so they can hear your thoughts and provide wisdom.

One practical step that both of you can take to make progress in this area is to read Song of Solomon separately and seek to model your thoughts, emotions, and desires after those of the king and his bride in that book. Does your love drip with the same language and feeling that those two lovers describe?

Clear a pathway in your thoughts. Sometimes we need to take our sexual thoughts about our spouses out of the freezer and place them on the counter to thaw. If you wait until the bedroom door is closed and locked to become aroused, it may take too long for you to get in the mood. Spend some time during the day longing for intimacy with your husband. Think about him throughout the day, and thank God for him. List all his pleasing qualities and characteristics, and stir up affections for him. Have holy, eager, and sensual thoughts exclusively for him.

If your mind has been occupied and distracted, it is time for you to clear a path (see Ps. 131). Don't allow clutter to accumulate. Talk with God about what is on your mind. Be anxious for nothing, but in everything by prayer and supplication with thanksgiving let your requests be made known to God (see Phil. 4:6). Lay all your tasks and troubles at the feet of Jesus so that you can lie fully with your husband.

Enjoy the freedom Jesus gives us as he takes our burdens (see Matt. 11:30; 2 Cor. 3:17). After offering your busy thoughts to God, be present in the moment with your husband. Be aware of him and set your eyes on him. Jim Elliot has said, "Wherever you are, be all there"[4]—and sex isn't excluded from this. When you are with your spouse, be all there.

A wife can and must be diligent to stay present mentally, physically, and emotionally while her husband is enjoying sex. This is not the time for her to review her task list or to think about every piece of her day. This is the time that she never gets back. It is the time for her to pause all else and glorify God with her husband in the marriage bed—as Scripture says, there is a time for everything (see Eccl. 3:1).

Your spouse will enjoy sex more if you do. Take your focus off your performance, and enjoy the experience. Some wives are so concerned about their husbands having a good time in bed that they can't enjoy the experience themselves. The irony is that most husbands love when their wives cut loose. Husbands love to know that their wives are thrilled and stimulated. Don't be so concerned about doing a great job; instead, be invested in having a great time.

Here is a handful of examples of thoughts you can put on to help you to cut loose.

- "I'm so thankful for my husband. Jesus, free me from a performance mentality and give me the power to love him well." See James 1:17.
- "I can be free from any standard of performance that the world imposes. When I delight in my husband, I fulfill my God-given role." See Song of Solomon 2:3.

4. Quoted in Elisabeth Elliot, *Through Gates of Splendor*, 25th Anniversary ed. (Carol Stream, IL: Tyndale Momentum, 1981), 20.

- "I can be comfortable with my body in the marriage bed because of the gospel. Jesus made a way for me to be bold despite my faults—to be naked and unashamed. I am flawed but very lovely." See Song of Solomon 1:2–5.
- "God created everything for me to enjoy. God, thank you for sex—and help us to be thrilled as I become unraveled in his arms." See Song of Solomon 2:16 and 7:13 as well as 1 Tim. 4:4.

Linger and love. Put away the clock and spend time together in bed. Husband, be patient with your wife and let love linger. Take the scenic highway instead of the interstate. The off road is winding, curvy, and fun, and you can experiment without pressure.[5] Pay no attention to the time or your speed—just linger and love.

Caress her wherever she feels most comfortable. Explore and experiment with stimulating her in ways that she enjoys. For example, speaking sweetly and genuinely while giving soft and sensual massages can be highly effective and is encouraged. Let her lead you, make suggestions, and invite you to all her intimate parts (see Song 4:16).

Changes in this area do not happen overnight. Putting off old anxious thoughts and putting on new hope-filled thoughts

---

5. Stuart Scott gives helpful advice to husbands about using self-control to prevent themselves from climaxing before their wives do. "Wait as long as possible in order to reach fulfillment together or bring your wife to fulfillment first. You and your wife both will experience far more enjoyment if you do not reach fulfillment before she does. . . . Husbands should not assume that caressing is enough to satisfy. Unless your wife communicates a lack of desire, always seek to bring her to *complete* fulfillment." Stuart Scott, *The Exemplary Husband: A Biblical Perspective*, rev. ed. (Bemidji, MN: Focus Publishing, 2002), 153.

takes time, grace, patience, and practice. As you start to make progress in this area, know that it is possible for a wife to experience deep sexual satisfaction in marriage. Sexual matters are important because they ultimately mirror the gospel. The perspective we have on sex and the way we practice it are connected to the way we understand and relate to God himself. Because of the freedom and forgiveness that we have in Jesus, we are able to boldly approach God and experience his pleasure (see Ps. 16:11; Heb. 4:16). This same kind of freedom and intimacy can characterize every marriage (see Gen. 2:25).[6]

God wants the garden of our bedroom to be pleasant and full of peace and to bloom with pleasure. These things are possible only through his power and presence.

Until then,
Sean and Jenny

DISCUSSION QUESTIONS

1. What are the factors (whether relational, personal, or medical) that you think could be contributing to your sexual difficulty?
2. If fear is a contributing factor, what passages of Scripture can help to renew your mind and put your fear to death?
3. What are some qualities and characteristics of your husband that you can enjoy and think about during the day?

6. See Perron, "On Sex," in Perron and Harmon, *Letters to a Romantic: On Engagement*, 107–12.

IMPURITY IN MARRIAGE

Sean and Jenny

Dear Romantic,

I cannot think of a deeper kind of betrayal than one that is committed by your most intimate companion.

Marriage is an exclusive covenant, and life and joy reside within it. When a spouse ventures outside this covenant, devastation and sadness result. Violating a vow brings pain. Grave harm results when the marriage bed is defiled.

A spouse can be impure in various ways—through lust, masturbation, homosexuality, physical adultery, inappropriate emotional relationships, pornography, sexting, and more. Whichever form impurity takes, its impact on the other spouse is real—and sin cannot be ignored.

TURNING TO GOD

All impurity is sin against God, and it brings about his wrath. The wrath that the sins of believers incur is satisfied through the death and resurrection of Jesus. For an unbeliever, though, that wrath is coming in full force: "Everyone who is sexually immoral or impure . . . has no inheritance in the kingdom of Christ and God. . . . Because of these things the wrath of God comes upon the sons of disobedience" (Eph. 5:5–6).

Although all impurity is sin, not every kind of impurity has the same results or requires the exact same steps of repentance. Still, all impurity calls for a response of godly sorrow,[1] faith, and repentance. Godly sorrow does not just mean feeling guilty or feeling bad for getting caught. It entails being sad about sinning against God, and it compels a person to repent—to turn away from sin and turn toward holiness.[2] When we sin, we have an advocate with the Father—and that is the best news in the whole world. Run to Jesus in faith, and you will find forgiveness (see 1 John 2:1).

Godly sorrow, faith, and repentance are the three minimum requirements for responding to impurity—but there are other steps to discuss taking as well.

SHOULD YOU CONFESS TO OTHERS?

Christians walk in the light (see John 8:12). The light is warm, bright, and clear. In it, you can see where you are going,

---

1. I highly recommend Heath Lambert's chapter on godly sorrow vs. worldly sorrow, chap. 3 in *Finally Free: Fighting for Purity with the Power of Grace* (Grand Rapids: Zondervan, 2013). Although the focus of this book is on pornography, you should read that chapter even if you have never struggled with that particular sin. It is worth the price of the book.

2. We are called to "bear fruit in keeping with repentance" as described in Matthew 3:8. "Repenting is what happens inside of us. Then this change leads to the fruits of new behavior. Repentance is not the new deeds, but the inward change that bears the fruit of new deeds. Jesus is demanding that we experience this inward change." John Piper, *What Jesus Demands from the World* (2006; repr., Wheaton, IL: Crossway, 2011), 41.

and others can see you. Nothing is hidden. If we walk in the light, as God is in the light, we have fellowship with one another, and the blood of Jesus cleanses us from all sin (see 1 John 1:7).

Sexual sin, in contrast, loves to hide in the darkness, because it can grow there unhindered. The false allure of an affair is thrilling—until someone is caught. The pleasure of pornography is enjoyable—until the shame of it is exposed. Sin hates the light, because confession exposes its lies and ugliness.

So when we are impure, we must both forsake our sin and come into the light. Believers *cannot* keep secret sins. We are compelled by the Holy Spirit to confess our sins and to get help if we have any pattern of sin in our lives. We are to expose our sin to the light and to others. "For at one time you were darkness, but now you are light in the Lord. Walk as children of light. . . . Take no part in the unfruitful works of darkness, but instead expose them" (Eph. 5:8, 11).

Who should you confess to?

Your spouse. If you have acted on a sinful sexual desire, you must confess this to your spouse—you have sinned against them and need to bring your sin into the light. You need their forgiveness in order to be in a right relationship with them.

Others who have been impacted by your sin. If your sin has impacted others, such as your relatives, your coworkers, or members of your church, then you must confess to them and ask their forgiveness as well. For example, if your children saw you flirting with another person, you must confess to them and explain that your actions were sinful.

An accountability partner. You should also share what has happened with a mature godly friend of the same gender. Confessing to a person like this is necessary if you are going to receive help and accountability (see James 5:16). You need to have someone who knows all your secrets—someone who knows your temptations, trials, and typical sins. It needs to be someone who is brutally honest with you and can exhort you in the faith (see Prov. 27:6). They need to be able to pray for you, speak into your life, and hold you accountable. You can have more than one person like this,[3] but you need at least one in your life. This relationship is crucial to your spiritual growth.

You must be transparent and vulnerable with this friend. If you have struggled with lust but not acted on it, this is the person to call. They should be aware of internal temptations you are experiencing or sins that haven't turned into actions.

It is wiser to share your internal sins with this friend instead of with your spouse. Your spouse doesn't need to know every time that you lust. That wouldn't be profitable for your relationship and would bog down your marriage in a way that would be unhealthy and unloving for your spouse. Knowing such details is a burden that your spouse shouldn't bear but that your friend should help you with.

Your spouse should, however, know that you have mature accountability partners. He or she should not be the one to "hold you accountable" but should know who is aware of your sin. They should be able to trust your accountability partners who are helping you with a plan of repentance. This will be a relief to your spouse.[4]

---

3. For example, don't be afraid to reach out to a pastor or minister at your local church as well. They would love to help you to repent and come alongside you.

4. A spouse who is struggling with understanding this concept should see the appendix for family members in Lambert, *Finally Free*.

HOW SHOULD YOU CONFESS?

Confessing sin is unpleasant, but it is life-giving. It shines a light upon the darkest parts of our hearts so that we can begin to become clean (see Eph. 5:12–13). How should we go about this process?

When you confess impurity to your spouse, you should give them enough information so that they will know what your sin was. If it was an affair, they need to know this. If it was pornography, then you need to say it was pornography. Explain the nature of the sin—but be careful about the details.[5]

It isn't helpful for a wife to hear what kinds of inappropriate photos her husband was looking at or for how long. It isn't helpful for a husband to know the sordid details of the weeklong affair his wife was having. Shameful details regarding sin don't need to be lodged in a spouse's mind. They will add a burden that the spouse will need grace to work through each time he or she remembers it. Instead, details like these should be shared with an accountability partner. Once this godly friend knows all these details, he or she can give advice on how much of them should be shared when a confession is made to the spouse.[6]

---

5. We outlined an approach that couples should take to disclosing their sexual history when they are dating in Sean Perron and Spencer Harmon, *Letters to a Romantic: On Dating* (Phillipsburg, NJ: P&R, 2017), 105–6, and the same basic principles of that approach apply here. When you confess impurity to your spouse, (1) pray, (2) invite a pastor or counselor, (3) consider what you will share, and (4) be patient. Sin can be shocking and painful. Your spouse may need time to pray and to reflect on Scripture while they process your confession.

6. If a physical act of sexual immorality has occurred, we always recommend that you involve a biblical counselor or pastor in your confession. Any attempt to confess and work through a sin of this nature must incorporate an accountability partner in the process to some extent, but some sins are

HOW SHOULD YOU RESPOND?

There is no way around it: betrayal is brutal. The pain from it can be deep and the recovery steep. But Jesus can redeem and restore all things.

No matter how major or horrible the impurity in your marriage has been, Jesus can overcome it.

Jesus knew the sting of traitors (see Ps. 55:12–23). One of his chosen companions turned against him. Judas ate bread with Jesus, as if nothing was wrong, and later kissed him like a friend during the height of his betrayal (see Matt. 26:21–25, 48–50). Peter also failed Jesus. He boldly declared that he would never deny him, but those words were empty. He denounced Jesus three times and was so passionate in his denial that he cursed (see Matt. 26:74). Even now, Jesus knows what it is like to have a beloved bride commit adultery against him (see James 4:4). We do it every day.

You and I have committed spiritual adultery against God by worshiping things that he has created (see Ezek. 16:30–43; Rom. 1:20–25; Col. 1:15–18; 3:5). At some point today, we have all loved an idol more than we've loved Jesus. The Bible calls this spiritual whoredom. We have all played the role of the harlot to our great God, and it grieves him when we do.

But the Lord is merciful, gracious, and abounding in steadfast love and forgiveness (see Ex. 34:6; Num. 14:18; Neh. 9:31; Ps. 86:5; Joel 2:13). He sets the example for how we should respond when our spouses confess to impurity. We must respond to such confessions with forgiveness, faithfulness, and hope for the future.

---

so sensitive and significant that a godly counselor should be involved in the confession itself—should be present before, during, and after it is made. If you don't know where to find a counselor, you can search for one at www .biblicalcounseling.com.

We must offer forgiveness, because we have received unparalleled forgiveness from God through the gospel (see Matt. 18:23–35) and because God calls us to have hearts that are free from bitterness. The only way we can forgive and be reconciled to our spouses is by understanding how much Christ has done for us through his sacrifice.

We must also continue to be faithful, because God is faithful—he will never leave us nor forsake us (see Heb. 13:5). He calls us to be faithful even when our spouses have been unfaithful. Even if things don't automatically return to normal immediately after an affair, we are to remain committed, compassionate, and kind to our spouses.[7] We are to follow the example of our God, who does not hold our sin against us.

Lastly, we are to believe that there is hope for the future. When our spouses confess, their sin is brought to light—and even though the light exposes painful realities, it also brings hope. There is no impurity that cannot be forgiven. There is no impurity that must destroy a marriage. Nothing is impossible or too hard for the Lord (see Matt. 19:26; Mark 14:36). If you are confronted with impurity, hold out hope for future restoration and pray for your marriage to be renewed.

If you have something to confess, now is the time. Awake, arise, and let Jesus shine upon you (see Eph. 5:13–14).

If you are receiving the news of a confession, hold out forgiveness and hope. No matter how dark things are, the darkness cannot overcome Christ and the light that he brings (see John 1:5).

Until then,
Sean and Jenny

7. For a helpful booklet on working through the aftermath of an affair,

DISCUSSION QUESTIONS

1. If you don't currently have a godly accountability partner, who is someone you can reach out to today?
2. Are there any secret sins that you need to confess to a godly accountability partner?
3. Are there any secret sins that you need to confess to your spouse?

see Robert D. Jones, *Restoring Your Broken Marriage: Healing after Adultery* (Greensboro, NC: New Growth Press, 2009).

FAITH AND REPENTANCE

Sean

Dear Romantic,

Too often we treat marriage like fireworks on the Fourth of July. We spend a bunch of money to have a big, bright celebration at the start. Bing. Bang. Boom. It is spectacular and expensive—but then we move on.

It's not meant to be this way. Marriage is a lifelong endeavor. Jesus doesn't want a firework show that fizzles. He wants candles that never go out. Our marriages are called to be a city on a hill whose lights come on every night (see Matt. 5:14–15). We are called to glow brighter than New York City on a clear night.

But how do we keep the glow of marriage going—how do we keep our marriages rich, meaningful, joyous, and flourishing? The answer might surprise you.

Faith and repentance.

Daily faith and repeated repentance make a marriage vibrant. They make it mesmerizing to the watching world. A marriage cannot last without daily faith and repentance.

CULTIVATE EVERYDAY FAITH AND REPENTANCE

To be a Christian is to be a lifelong disciple, and to be a disciple is to decide every day to pursue faith and repentance. In Luke 9:23, Jesus makes this clear when he says, "If anyone would come after me, let him deny himself and take up his cross daily and follow me."

Let's see how this applies to your marriage.

Desire to follow Jesus. Do you want your marriage to glow for the glory of God? You must have a sincere desire to follow Jesus throughout your marriage. If you don't have this desire, Jesus will be an afterthought. Your life will be choked by the cares of the world instead of gripped by the cares of Christ (see Matt. 13:7, 22). Does Jesus captivate you? If he doesn't first captivate you and your spouse personally and internally, he won't captivate your marriage. If the desires of the world take hold of your marriage, you will be susceptible to temptation—to immorality and unfaithfulness (see 1 John 2:15–17). Your desire is linked to your faith. When you believe that Jesus is the most precious thing in life and in death, your desire for him will increase.

Deny yourself. Once you have desired to follow Jesus, you must deny yourself. You must keep your selfish desires from ruling your life. Christians have new hearts (see Col. 3:10), but we do not have perfect hearts. Our hearts still possess sinful inclinations that need to be denied. Repenting from sinful desires means saying no to your sin and yes to God's righteousness. It means putting off sin and putting on Christ by faith. Through faith we trust that God is more satisfying, more enjoyable, more thrilling, and more rewarding than sin.

Your marriage will provide you with countless opportunities

to put your preferences to death. You will want to be right during arguments. You will want to control your finances your way. You will want to spend time with your in-laws on your terms. You must decide every day to deny yourself, or you will continually be self-centered. Self-absorbed spouses make sour marriages.

Die to sin daily. Repenting means putting sin to death (see Rom. 8:13; Col. 3:5). We must kill sin. Crush it. Crucify it. We must put ourselves—our preferences, wants, idols, and selfish desires—to death. This will require us to be intentional. It will take an act of the will (see Phil. 2:12–13). Pick up your cross, and don't allow sin to remain in your marriage. Whatever your sin is—laziness, lust, dishonesty, or anything else—you must lay it in the grave. You must by faith consider yourself to be dead to sin but alive to God in Christ Jesus (see Rom. 6:11).

The reason you can pick up your cross and follow Jesus is because he first picked up his cross for you. Jesus died and rose again to not only take away the penalty of your sin but also to give you power over your sin. We gain the power to obey God through faith in Jesus.

Every dawn, you need to crucify your preferences by grace and through faith. This is the daily pattern of the Christian marriage. Each sunrise should involve your putting sin to death. You must turn away from sin today, tomorrow, the next day, and the day after that (see 1 Cor. 15:31)—for year one, year two, year five, and year fifty. The life that we now live, we live by faith in the Son of God who loved us and gave himself for us (see Gal. 2:20).

Devote yourself to God. After we die to ourselves, we must be devoted to each other and to God. We are to put off the old and put on the new (see Eph. 4:22, 24). We must bear fruit in keeping with repentance (see Matt. 3:8). It isn't enough for us to deny our sinful desires; we have to cultivate righteous desires.

We must replace selfish lust with selfless love. We must pursue thankfulness instead of covetousness. We must offer grace rather than judgement. We must extend kindness in the place of harshness. Jesus wants couples to clothe themselves in humility and in genuine affection for each other. They are to be truly and uniquely devoted to each other in love.

WHERE THE CROSS MEETS THE PAVEMENT

Daily faith and repentance get very practical in a marriage. Let's say you are coming home from work after a long day and are dragging. You know that when you get home your wife will want to tell you about her day, and that you will have to listen to everything that has happened to her, when all you want is to kick back with a drink and watch your favorite series. Instead, you need to desire Christ, deny yourself, die to sin, and devote yourself to God.

Your commute home can be a great opportunity for you to focus on *desiring* to follow Jesus rather than following your own agenda. Believe, by faith, that obedience to God brings joy. When you are tempted to take it easy, it is time for you to *deny* yourself and kill your lazy inclinations. Make them *die*. Instead of checking out, it is time for you to check in. You can ask God, by faith, for the grace to *devote* yourself to your spouse. You can put on selfless love. And then, when you open the door to your house, be there. Be on. Be ready. Squeeze your wife's hand, listen to her share about her day, and then tell her all about yours. Find joy in losing your life for the sake of your wife.

Or maybe you receive a phone call from your husband. He breaks the news to you that he has lost his credit card for the second time. He already lost his driver's license last month, which meant you had to deal with the DMV. Now you have to cancel the credit card yet again and wait for a new one to come in the mail before you can buy groceries.

This phone call is a moment for you to desire Christ, deny yourself, die to sin, and devote yourself to God and to your spouse. Instead of unleashing on your husband, you can *desire* to respect him and to honor God. Instead of giving in to the self-righteous impulse to say "I told you so," you can *deny* it. Put your lecture to *death*, and put on love. By grace, and through faith, you can *devote* yourself to sympathizing with your husband's situation. Ask God to help you to repent and to deliver a kind word that will be full of forgiveness instead of bitterness.

LOSE YOUR LIFE TO SAVE YOUR MARRIAGE

All this talk about denying and dying might seem dark and gloomy. But it isn't.

Death each dawn brings about light each night.

A denial of selfish desires resembles the winter that brings about spring.

Repeated faith and repentance reap life: "Truly, truly, I say to you, unless a grain of wheat falls into the earth and dies, it remains alone; but if it dies, it bears much fruit" (John 12:24).

Are you willing to lose your life today in order to "save" your marriage? What about tomorrow?

I promise that you won't regret it.

Until then,
Sean

DISCUSSION QUESTIONS

1. How often do you think about the gospel (Jesus's life, death, and resurrection for sinners) during your week?
2. What are some ways that you need to "die" in your marriage?
3. What are some things that your spouse would like for you to "put to death"?

CONCLUSION

UNTIL THEN

Sean and Spencer

Dear Romantic,

When each of us comes home from work, a predictable series of events takes place.

I (Sean) open the door and hear the hum of the dryer mixed with the beeps and jingles of Chandler's toys.

I then hear Jenny gasp and say something like "Daddy's home! Go get Daddy!" Chandler giggles and comes running around the corner or down the hall, ready to show me a block or a random kitchen utensil that has remarkably turned fun. I tickle Chandler till he squeals with laughter and greet Jenny with a kiss, and we proceed to make dinner or go on a walk while we catch up on the day. We chat and do chores until the bed beckons, and then we call it a night.

I (Spencer) open the door, put down my bag, and more often than not become immediately engaged in a game of hide-and-seek as I try to find where my girls are hiding from me. After I find them under my covers or in a closet, they squeal and say,

"You're home!" I kiss my wife as she holds our son. We make dinner, play for a while, and then wind down for the night.

Our ordinary days are full of extraordinary moments.

Marriage isn't meant to be one gigantic, escalating thrill ride. Instead, it's designed by God to consist of normal days that are filled with wonder and glory. Throughout those normal days, we are being conformed to the image of his Son, which will continue until that day when we see him face-to-face.

That's why every letter we have written you ends with the same two words: "Until then."

When you are preparing for marriage, "then" is the big moment when you covenant your life to your spouse—when you finally say "I do" surrounded by friends and family. The wedding altar feels like the finish line—like the rightful conclusion to a season. On your wedding day, "until then" fades into "now."

So what does "then" refer to now that your wedding is over—when we write "until then," when do we mean?

We mean the day of the greater marriage from which our marriages all take their cues. Paul describes that greater marriage in a beautiful passage in Ephesians:

> Christ loved the church and gave himself up for her, that he might sanctify her, having cleansed her by the washing of water with the word, so that he might present the church to himself in splendor, without spot or wrinkle or any such thing, that she might be holy and without blemish. (Eph. 5:25–27)

Every Christian marriage is leading to this moment. The moment when we are presented to Jesus, with the rest of his church, in splendor—without spot or wrinkle—holy and blameless. This is the great hope that we carry throughout our marriages and the fuel that sustains us every day. We strive to grow, by grace, slowly and surely, so that we will look more and more like the people we will be on this last day (see 2 Cor. 3:18).

On that day, the picture will melt into reality—Jesus's church will be presented to him as his bride (see Rev. 21:1–2), and we will be with our Savior forever. This is the great marriage that we hope in and aim to grow toward. It is this great day that strengthens us throughout the first years of marriage and every year afterward.

Until then, we love our spouses sacrificially and grow through the grace of Christ. Until then, we believe the gospel afresh each morning and confess every sin that seeks to ensnare us. Until then, we devotedly pursue our spouses. Until then, we apply God's Word to every nook and cranny of our lives. Until then, we hope in the glory of God during each ordinary day and extraordinary moment.

May your marriage always have that great day in view when every tear will be wiped away, the curse will be undone, death will be no more, and all things will be made new by King Jesus. His Word is true (see Prov. 30:5–6). He won't put us to shame (see Rom. 10:11). He gives us everything that we need.

Abide in Jesus—today, and tomorrow, and until then,
Sean and Spencer

ACKNOWLEDGMENTS

The writing process for this third book in the *Letters to a Romantic* series has felt vastly different from the process for the previous two books. Our season of life is now different, our jobs are different, and our homes have new additions! This book would not have existed if it hadn't been for the help of our friends, our families, and our church. And Jesus deserves the most praise for his grace and for placing everyone in our lives who made this work possible.

Our wives have been 100 percent supportive and have sacrificed their precious time to help to complete this project. First Baptist Church of Jacksonville has encouraged us and celebrated with us. We want to specifically thank the Lamberts and the Youngs for doing our premarriage counseling and for introducing us to many of the ideas in this book and helping us to instill them in our own homes. If a reader finds something helpful in this book, it probably originated from them! On top of this, our parents (and grandparents) have been praying at every turn, and we are eager to see God answer their prayers by transforming lives.

We want to give a special thanks to the following people who have helped with the manuscript in various ways. These people include Caroline Haley, Josie Padilla, David and Jordan

Burdetsky, Stephen and Isabella Schumacher, Taron and Kristen Defevers, and Trevor and Amber Komatsu. We'd also like to thank Martha Peace and Stuart Scott for supporting this work with their kind introduction. We also want to thank the crew at P&R for all their support! Amanda Martin, Dave Almack, Rush Witt, Aaron Gottier, and Ian Thompson are a joy to work with, and we are eternally grateful for them.

RECOMMENDED RESOURCES

ESSENTIAL READING ON MARRIAGE

Harvey, Dave. *When Sinners Say "I Do": Discovering the Power of the Gospel for Marriage*. Wapwallopen, PA: Shepherd Press, 2007.

Peace, Martha. *The Excellent Wife: A Biblical Perspective*. Bemidji, MN: Focus Publishing, 1995.

Piper, John. *This Momentary Marriage: A Parable of Permanence*. 2009. Reprint, Wheaton, IL: Crossway, 2012.

Scott, Stuart. *The Exemplary Husband: A Biblical Perspective*. Rev. ed. Bemidji, MN: Focus Publishing, 2002.

Tripp, Paul David. *What Did You Expect? Redeeming the Realities of Marriage*. Wheaton, IL: Crossway, 2010

DAILY DEVOTIONALS TO ENJOY TOGETHER

Bridges, Jerry. *31 Days toward Trusting God*. 2013. Reprint, Colorado Springs: NavPress, 2017.

Newheiser, Jim. *Money: Seeking God's Wisdom*. 31-Day Devotionals for Life. Phillipsburg, NJ: P&R Publishing, 2019.

Scott, Stuart, with S. Andrew Jin. *31 Ways to Be a "One-Another" Christian: Loving Others with the Love of Jesus*. Wapwallopen, PA: Shepherd Press, 2019.

Tripp, Paul David. *New Morning Mercies: A Daily Gospel Devotional.* Wheaton, IL: Crossway, 2014.

Welch, Edward T. *A Small Book about a Big Problem: Meditations on Anger, Patience, and Peace.* Greensboro, NC: New Growth Press, 2017.

———. *A Small Book for the Anxious Heart: Meditations on Fear, Worry, and Trust.* Greensboro, NC: New Growth Press, 2019.

FURTHER RESOURCES BY TOPIC

Abuse

Gannon, Pamela, and Beverly Moore. *In the Aftermath: Past the Pain of Childhood Sexual Abuse.* Bemidji, MN: Focus Publishing, 2017.

Lambert, Heath. "Restoration After Abuse." Produced by Association of Certified Biblical Counselors. *Truth in Love*, December 22, 2016. Podcast, mp3 audio, 15:04. https://biblicalcounseling. com/restoration-abuse-transcript/.

Lambert, Heath, with Timothy Pasma. "Emotional Abuse." Produced by Association of Certified Biblical Counselors. *Truth in Love*, October 13, 2017. Podcast, mp3 audio, 7:55. https://biblical counseling.com/til-135/.

Moles, Chris. *The Heart of Domestic Abuse: Gospel Solutions for Men Who Use Control and Violence in the Home.* Bemidji, MN: Focus Publishing, 2015.

Newheiser, Jim. *Help! Someone I Love Has Been Abused.* Wapwallopen, PA: Shepherd Press, 2014.

Conflict

Baker, Ernie. *Help! I'm in a Conflict.* Wapwallopen, PA: Shepherd Press, 2015.

Jones, Robert D. *Pursuing Peace: A Christian Guide to Handling Our Conflicts.* Wheaton, IL: Crossway, 2012.

Lambert, Heath. "Should I Forgive Someone Who's Not Sorry They Sinned?" Produced by Association of Certified Biblical Counselors. *Truth in Love*, September 29, 2016. Podcast, mp3 audio, 9:30. https://biblicalcounseling.com/forgive-someone-whos-not-sorry-sinned-transcript/.

Sande, Ken, with Tom Raabe. *Peacemaking for Families: A Biblical Guide to Managing Conflict in Your Home.* Carol Stream, IL: Tyndale House, 2002.

Family and Home

Alcorn, Randy. *The Treasure Principle: Discovering the Secret of Joyful Giving.* Colorado Springs: Multnomah, 2001.

Butterfield, Rosaria. *The Gospel Comes with a House Key: Practicing Radically Ordinary Hospitality in Our Post-Christian World.* Wheaton, IL: Crossway, 2018.

Strachan, Owen, and Gavin Peacock. *The Grand Design: Male and Female He Made Them.* Rev. ed. Fearn, UK: Christian Focus, 2016.

Family and Parenting

Gibson, Jonathan. *The Moon Is Always Round.* Greensboro, NC: New Growth Press, 2019.

Tautges, Paul, and Karen Tautges. *Help! My Toddler Rules the House.* Wapwallopen, PA: Shepherd Press, 2014.

Tripp, Tedd. *Shepherding a Child's Heart.* Wapwallopen, PA: Shepherd Press, 1995.

Whitney, Donald S. *Family Worship.* Wheaton, IL: Crossway, 2016.

Intimacy and Sexual Issues

Burk, Denny, and Heath Lambert. *Transforming Homosexuality: What the Bible Says about Sexual Orientation and Change.* Phillipsburg, NJ: P&R, 2015.

Lambert, Heath. *Finally Free: Fighting for Purity with the Power of Grace.* Grand Rapids: Zondervan, 2013.

Lambert, Heath, with Brad Bigney. "Glorifying God In Your Sexual Relationship." Produced by Association of Certified Biblical Counselors. *Truth in Love,* April 5, 2017. Podcast, mp3 audio, 13:14. https://biblicalcounseling.com/til-087-glorifying-god -sexual-relationship-feat-brad-bigney/

Mahaney, C. J. *Sex, Romance, and the Glory of God: What Every Christian Husband Needs to Know.* Wheaton, IL: Crossway, 2004.

Street, John D. *Passions of the Heart: Biblical Counsel for Stubborn Sexual Sins.* Phillipsburg, NJ: P&R, 2019.

Wheat, Ed, and Gaye Wheat. *Intended for Pleasure: Sex Technique and Sexual Fulfillment in Christian Marriage.* 4th ed. Grand Rapids: Revell, 2010.

Trials

Bridges, Jerry. *Trusting God.* 1988. Reprint, Colorado Springs: NavPress, 2016.

Jones, Robert D. *Restoring Your Broken Marriage: Healing after Adultery.* Greensboro, NC: New Growth Press, 2009.

Piper, John. *Don't Waste Your Cancer.* Wheaton, IL: Crossway, 2011.

———. *Lessons from a Hospital Bed.* Wheaton, IL: Crossway, 2016.

Tautges, Paul. *A Small Book for the Hurting Heart: Meditations on Loss, Grief, and Healing.* Greensboro, NC: New Growth Press, 2020.

Vroegop, Mark. *Dark Clouds, Deep Mercy: Discovering the Grace of Lament.* Wheaton, IL: Crossway, 2019.

Personal Spiritual Growth

Bridges, Jerry. *The Discipline of Grace.* Updated ed. Colorado Springs: NavPress, 2006.

Chester, Tim. *You Can Change: God's Transforming Power for Our Sinful Behavior and Negative Emotions.* Wheaton, IL: Crossway, 2010.

Leeman, Jonathan. *Church Membership: How the World Knows Who Represents Jesus.* Wheaton, IL: Crossway, 2012.

Rigney, Joe. *The Things of Earth: Treasuring God by Enjoying His Gifts.* Wheaton, IL: Crossway, 2015.

Vincent, Milton. *A Gospel Primer for Christians: Learning to See the Glories of God's Love.* Bemidji, MN: Focus Publishing, 2008.

FINDING A COUNSELOR

If you are looking for further help, you can find a certified biblical counselor at www.biblicalcounseling.com. Every certified counselor with the Association of Certified Biblical Counselors (ACBC) is trained in marriage counseling, and numerous counselors specialize in this area and give a large portion of their ministry to helping marriages.

Sean Perron (MDiv, The Southern Baptist Theological Seminary) is the associate pastor at First Baptist Church in Jacksonville, Florida. He is a certified biblical counselor who has a specialization in marriage counseling, and he was previously the director of operations at the Association of Certified Biblical Counselors (ACBC). He and his wife, Jennifer, have one son.

Spencer Harmon serves as the campus pastor at First Baptist Church's Nocatee Campus in Jacksonville, Florida. He and his wife, Taylor, live in Saint Johns, Florida, and have two daughters and one son.

Together Sean and Spencer write on their website: www.unspokenblog.com.

Did you find this book helpful?
Consider writing a review online.
The author appreciates your feedback!

Or write to P&R at editorial@prpbooks.com
with your comments. We'd love to hear from you.

Association of Certified
Biblical Counselors

Since 1976, the Association of Certified Biblical Counselors (ACBC) has been training and certifying biblical counselors to ensure excellence in the counseling room by faithfulness to the Word of God. We offer a comprehensive biblical counseling certification program that is rigorous, but attainable by even the busiest pastor or church member. Our certification process is made up of three phases: learning, exams and application, and supervision.

ACBC has grown from a handful of individuals to thousands of certified counselors all around the world. Now in our fourth decade of pursuing excellence in biblical counseling, we have had five executive directors: Dr. Bob Smith, Dr. Howard Eyrich, Rev. Bill Goode, and Rev. Randy Patten. Dr. Heath Lambert became the fifth executive director in 2013.

Every Christian is called to speak the truth in love to one another. ACBC trains Christians in their gospel responsibility to be disciple-makers and to build up the body of Christ. This training is accomplished through conferences and events throughout the world.

For more information about ACBC and biblical counseling resources, visit www.biblicalcounseling.com.

Christian couples need to be reminded regularly of the basics of a Christian marriage. In a clear, down-to-earth style, Martha Peace and John Crotts provide these reminders through short chapters that couples can read, study, and pray over together. Each section ends with two recommended resources for readers who want to dig deeper in a particular area.

"There are many uses—both personal and pastoral—for this practical little book. In the home, for example, it can be adapted easily for family worship. In the church it can serve as a useful resource for counseling, as a tool for a marriage retreat, and more."

—**Don Whitney**, *The Southern Baptist Theological Seminary*

ALSO BY SEAN PERRON & SPENCER HARMON

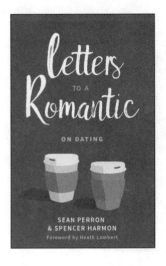 

"Wow! What a needed resource for single men and women. Dating can be one of the most confusing times in a single person's life, and we desperately need solid biblical guidance in this area. Thank you, Sean and Spencer, for giving us this incredibly practical and biblical book on dating. We highly recommend it!"

—**Kristen Clark and Bethany Baird**, Founders, Girl-Defined Ministries

"Engagement is an exhilarating step toward the unknown with someone you're still getting to know. Where can a couple get wise counsel for a season that ricochets, almost daily, between sparkling anticipation and disorienting discussion? The answer is two guys and a book. . . . You will come away packed with fresh faith, enriched by practical insights, and uniquely prepared for the magnificent journey toward marriage!"

—**Dave Harvey**, Executive Director, Sojourn Network

BY MARTHA PEACE AND STUART SCOTT

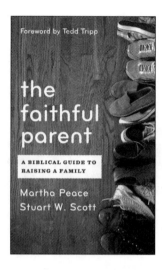

Martha Peace, best-selling author of *The Excellent Wife*, and Stuart Scott, author of its counterpart, *The Exemplary Husband*, join forces to challenge you to become a faithful parent—one who perseveres and leaves the results to God.

"The book you are holding is an outstanding resource. The authors are seasoned Christians who are safe spiritual guides. They are full of the hope and grace of the gospel. They are wise in their understanding of the nature of the Christian life. They are insightful in their understanding of the needs of children and the difficulties of being a faithful parent. They are mature in their application of the Bible and its message to the challenges of raising children. This will be a timeless resource."
—**Tedd Tripp**, Author, *Shepherding a Child's Heart*